To Mervyn,
On the occasion of
your 60th Birthday.

Private Thoughts
from a Small Shoot

Best wishes

Ashley R Ba—

Also published by Merlin Unwin Books
7 Corve Street, Ludlow, Shropshire SY8 1DB, U.K.

CONFESSIONS OF A SHOOTING FISHING MAN
Laurence Catlow £9.99 Pb

ONCE A FLYFISHER
Laurence Catlow £17.99 Hb

THE ONE THAT GOT AWAY
tales of days when fish triumphed over anglers
Jeremy Paxman, George Melly, David Steel, et al £16.95 Hb

THE FAR FROM COMPLEAT ANGLER
Tom Fort £16.99 Hb

BRIGHT WATERS a celebration of Irish fishing
Niall Fallon & Tom Fort £20 Hb

THE DRY FLY
Conrad Voss Bark £20 Hb

TROUT & SALMON FLIES OF IRELAND
Peter O'Reilly £20 Hb

RIVERS OF IRELAND
a flyfisher's guide, 5th edition
Peter O' Reilly £20 Hb

LOUGHS OF IRELAND
a flyfisher's guide, 3rd edition
Peter O' Reilly £17.99 Hb

A HISTORY OF FLYFISHING
Conrad Voss Bark £25 Hb/£12.95 Pb

AN ANGLER FOR ALL SEASONS
the best of H.T.Sheringham £16.95 Hb

BEGINNER'S GUIDE TO FLYTYING
Chris Mann & Terry Griffiths £7.99 Hb

FALLING IN AGAIN
tales of an incorrigible angler
Chris Yates £17.99 Hb

THE SECRET CARP
Chris Yates £17.99 Hb

PRIVATE THOUGHTS
FROM A SMALL SHOOT

Laurence Catlow

Illustrated by Ashley Boon

MERLIN UNWIN BOOKS

First published in Great Britain by Merlin Unwin Books, 2003
Text copyright © Laurence Catlow, 2003
Illustrations copyright © Ashley Boon, 2003

MERLIN UNWIN BOOKS
7 Corve Street, Ludlow
Shropshire SY8 1DB, U.K.
Tel 01584 877456
Fax 01584 877457
email: books@merlinunwin.co.uk
website: www.merlinunwin.co.uk

British Library Cataloguing in Publication Data:
A catalogue record for this book is available from the British Library

ISBN 1-873674-68-6

Designed and typeset by Merlin Unwin Books, Ludlow, UK.
Printed in Great Britain by Biddles Ltd, Kings Lynn

CONTENTS

CHAPTER ONE

JULY

Right to roam; my beautiful pheasant
shoot; Catlow the fisherman; shooting
experience; appraising the dogs

Not long ago – it was early in June and the sun was shining – I spent the afternoon wandering round my little farm. There are just over fifty acres of it and, as far as I am concerned, it is the centre of the world, lying up there on the edge of the Pennines not far from a little village called Brough. There are just over fifty acres of it, with perhaps another thirty where I have permission to go exploring with my dogs and my gun; but it is those fifty acres that really matter to me. They are all mine, those fifty acres are; they are my kingdom, my pride and my joy; they are my pheasant shoot, and it does not bother me a fig that fifty acres are too few for anything but a very rough and ready sort of pheasant shoot. They are a place for me and for my dogs and for my friends; we are all perfectly content with a rough and ready sort of pheasant shoot; they are a private place and I rejoice that there is no right of way over a single square inch of any one of my fifty acres.

I do not want half the world tramping over my little kingdom. I want most people nowhere near it. I want to share it with just a few

kindred spirits; and so when spirits not on the list suggest to me that this is an exclusive and selfish attitude, I suggest to them that they should grant me unconfined access to their gardens and their garages and their bedrooms. They always tell me that their garages and their gardens, not to mention their bedrooms, are a different matter altogether. I cannot see how; private property, it seems to me, is private property, whether or not it is enclosed by a neatly clipped privet hedge or thickly carpeted or sheltered from the elements by four walls and a slated roof. But I let the matter drop, happy to leave other men in unchallenged possession of their little kingdoms, as long as they, however grudgingly, are willing to leave me in freedom to enjoy the seclusion of my own.

I did not start these pages with the intention of announcing to the nation that, with very few exceptions, it is unwelcome on my fifty acres. I intended to celebrate rather than to exclude: to celebrate the loveliness of my fifty acres and to revel in their beauty. The other day they looked very beautiful indeed. The meadow was full of waving grass and the grass was full of bright flowers, of orchids and yellow rattle, of buttercups and tall daisies, of clover and red sorrel and purple splashes of bistort. I was walking along the edge of the meadow and, above me on the left, all the young ashes and oaks and hazels and wild cherries that I planted three years ago were waving their leaves above the tops of their tubes; and the aspen saplings, which sprang up everywhere on the Rise as soon as it was fenced off, the aspens were all swaying and shining in the breeze and the bright light.

At the top of the Rise there is an old hedge of holly and hazel, of ash and hawthorn; there is a ditch in the shadow of this hedge, choked with rushes and with rough grass. As I walked along the edge of the meadow the other day, looking up towards the line of the hedge, briefly my mind wandered away from summer, wandering off to frosty mornings in December and to the pheasants

that, come next winter, will surely spring from the ditch where they love to hide, flying high over the meadow in search of shelter on Beck. Bank Sometimes they climb all the way and are fine birds when they cross the guns.

My beck is really called a sike. There are many sikes in this part of Cumbria and, should you be interested in such things, the dictionary tells me that the word is from the old Norse. My beck even has a name; it is called Powbrand Sike and it flows straight down the steep little valley that forms the heart of my shoot; then, when my valley begins to spread itself, the sike slants across the top of the meadow, dividing the flat land where the hay grows from the rough and rising ground on the southern side; it turns against a high bank, from the top of which an old oak leans way out over the water. Then the stream splits, forming a little island where a few straggling gorse bushes have decided to grow; then it turns again and flows over my boundary towards its junction with the Bela about a mile away.

The other day the beck was full and clear, with wild roses bending over the water and spilling their white petals into the stream. Beck Bank is densely overgrown with hawthorns and brambles and impenetrable thickets of blackthorn. On the slope there are a few ashes and a few taller oaks; up on top, just over the fence that marks the limit of my land, rise three or four noble Scots pines and a line of tall, silver-trunked beeches.

Beck Bank is a problem. There is a small stand of Douglas firs at its lower and flatter end on the edge of the water, with a planting of larches at its eastern limit above the meadow gate. My pheasants love the Douglas firs and the larches and the tangled cover all over the slope. They also love to fly the wrong way when flushed, or to run out at the top corner in order to avoid being flushed at all. I have plans for the coming season, but I shall wait to explain them until the season has moved a little nearer. The other day there was a

blackcap singing somewhere in the hawthorns on Beck Bank; there was a woodpecker drumming in the firs and a cock pheasant shouting from the edge of the larches.

I went through the meadow gate, past the hedge where we eat our sandwiches on shooting days, sitting there with perhaps a dozen pheasants and a few rabbits lying somewhere near us on the bank, with our dogs waiting to be rewarded for their work in the morning: for those four cocks that Austin's Meg put over the guns back in the wood, for the runner that my Merlin brought in at last when we had all decided that it would never be found, for pheasants and rabbits flushed from spiky jungles of gorse, from dense and tearing clumps of thorns and brambles, from rush-choked ditches and from all those matted and tangled places in which my shoot abounds.

I went through the gate and walked along the bottom of the steep bank of gorse that rises on the left. The other day the bank was still yellow with flowers. It makes two little drives on pheasant days; one is called the Whins, the other the Gutter: a long, deep ditch, thick with gorse from top to bottom, that runs down to the sike from my northern boundary. Sometimes, especially during hard weather, they are productive little drives; there are also days when they do not put a single pheasant into the sky. There was one morning last season when the Gutter was full of birds, which rose into a bullying wind that swept them high over the sike. Not many of them fell.

I did not go up through the gorse the other day. I crossed the sike just in front of the patch of flat ground that is the best place for a standing gun when the dogs are busy on Beck Bank. It is right on the edge of the water, and it is the sound of water that you hear as you stand there waiting, until suddenly there is a pheasant above you in the sky and there is barely time for you to mount your gun. I crossed the sike, remembering the four birds I shot there on my

November shoot last year; then I walked up the open ground of Pheasant Hill where, seeing a few primroses still in bloom, I forgot about last November and gave myself over to the pleasures of June. There were two buzzards soaring high above me, mewing and circling on their broad wings; they make me nervous when my pens are full of poults, but at all other times I enjoy their presence over my land. Owls often nest in the wood and sometimes a pair of sparrow hawks; owls and sparrow hawks have helped themselves to more of my poults than the buzzards have ever done.

The old pen is up the hill and just inside the trees. I went there to inspect the wire and decide how much of it needed replacing. The pen has been there for eight years now; it is on a slope, and the wire on the bottom side, as the weight of earth and stones and rotting leaves builds up behind it, is beginning to bulge and tear. Next year may be the time to rebuild it; this year I think an afternoon's work, full of sweat and midges, will be enough to make it secure again. After deciding this I sat in the sunshine above the pen and smoked for five minutes; I watched a red squirrel bound away from me through the trees; briefly I looked forward to those August days that will be spent watering and feeding birds, hanging hoppers and filling them, setting and checking my traps, lying in ambush for the crows that will start descending from the sky in black hordes to stuff themselves on my grain. There is plenty to be done at High Park in August; but it is always good to rest for a while at the end of another afternoon's work, lying back in the sun and listening to the sound of gorse pods popping in the August heat.

I did not get round all my fifty acres the other day; I walked along my top ground above the wood, a long strip of open land between the edge of the trees and the boundary fence, rushy land with dense tangles of briars and haws and brambles. This is where my best pheasants rise. Merlin flushes them from the rushes and the brambles; some fly over the boundary fence and are crossing targets

for my gun. These are just ordinary birds, but others swing to the right and fly over the steep sides of the wood, high over the sike where my friends are waiting with their boots in running water. They are fine fast birds and you must get onto them very quickly.

I wandered into the wood itself, where willow warblers and wrens and chaffinches were singing away. My wood has a name as well as my sike; it is called Brogden's Plantation, and I have no idea who Brogden was or if it was he who planted it. To my eyes it does not look like a plantation at all, but like a little remnant of the wild wood; it is mostly hazel and birch, with a few oaks and ashes and dead elms down by the water. It was coppiced once and I should like to coppice it again; but there are sheep in the wood until August and, although they avoid the steeper parts – which means most of it – and although they browse mostly on the edges, you cannot coppice a wood where sheep roam. I cannot afford to fence off the wood and so the sheep will stay until I have turned into a rich man. Given the presence of the sheep there is a surprising amount of cover in Brogden's Plantation.

As I walked through my wood the other day I saw a brood of pheasants scampering ahead of me to take shelter in the rushes. I counted seven or eight of them and wondered how many would survive into the coming winter. Reaching my eastern boundary I went down along the rickety fence, through the hazels and the birches, down to the sike and the deep shadows at the bottom of the slope. I began to follow the stream back though the wood, squelching through the marshy land in the narrow bottom, skirting the rotting trunks of fallen elms, watching a few rabbits running ahead of me and a pigeon or two clattering from the trees.

Down in the bottom of the wood in high summer, down there by the sike, it is always damp and green and full of shadows; there are ferns on the edge of the water and there is moss on the fallen

trunks and branches and on all the rotting stumps; but even in high summer I never walk there beneath the dense cover of the leaves without thinking of the same place in pheasant time, in November and, better still, in December and January, when all the trees are bare except for those clusters of shrivelled brown leaves hanging from the branches of oaks, and for those polished and pointed green leaves on the hollies, except for these and the twining masses of ivy round so many of the birches; and though it may be June with a hot sun shining above the leaves, I think of frost sharp on the winter air and deep in the cold ground, I think of pheasants crouching in piles of brash and in the dense thickets of gorse that extend along the edge of the trees on top of the valley's northern slope; my mind's eye sees dogs hunting up and down the slope, with guns waiting on the edge of the sike, until all at once the first pheasant comes gliding silently over the trees. This little drive is called North Bank and it is, I think, the most dependable drive on my little shoot.

I did not go up to the high ground of my faraway, up above the gorse to the rushes where the rabbits squat. Occasionally we find a hare there as well, but, although I love the rich flavour of their flesh, hares are now a rare presence on my ground and they are no longer shot. I left the Ten Acre unvisited and the Middle Pasture below it and the Stackhole beyond; they are all rushy fields and they are always worth a walk on shooting days; rabbits are their usual contribution to the bag, but there is often a pheasant or two and sometimes a woodcock, with more rarely a snipe from the marshy ground in the Stackhole below the spring.

I did not even go up to the New Pen in the fenced-off strip above the Whins, although mention of it reminds me of a December pheasant that rose from the edge of the wire and kept rising until he had flown over four standing guns, too high and too fast for all four of them; and the sun was shining on him as he flew and it was very beautiful to see. Last season was the first with the New Pen; but

already I have learned from experience and I shall be surprised if, during the coming season, I cannot exploit its presence more successfully. After the first shoot or two I think the strip to which it belongs will be better driven with walking guns ten yards below the fence rather than with standing guns waiting down below the gorse on the edge of the sike.

I left the New Pen unvisited and came back down to the sike through a gap in the gorse, seeing at once that the rides we cut two or three years ago now need clearing again, and that both the Whins and the Gutter would benefit from more brutal and extensive assault with loppers and strimmers and saws. They would still hold plenty of birds and, with more gaps and clearings in the gorse, I fancy our

dogs would manage to put more of them onto the wing. I did not promise to get it all done this summer, though I told myself that it would be a good idea to make a start. The rides, at least, must be made easily passable again. Next Lent, I decided, would be the time for a really savage attack; for gorse, as you probably know – unless you set fire to it and burn it to the ground – gorse resists any attempt to take back even a portion of the land it has claimed for itself; it resents all efforts at control or management; it pricks and pierces the man who would hack it down; it scratches and tears him, so that every yard, every foot of progress exacts its sharp price of suffering and pain; and it leaves its spikes in gloves and stockings and flesh, waiting there to wound the enemy when he thinks the day's struggle is at last over; there is something penitential about time spent in intimate contact with gorse; it is an ideal activity for Lent.

I sat down when I came back to the water, somewhat relieved that I had just postponed any serious gorse management for almost a year. I sat down, lit my pipe and enjoyed the feel of the summer sun and the sight of a clump of ragged robin, with pink flowers waving and straggling on their stalks above a patch of boggy ground. I rarely go to High Park without sitting for a few minutes and marvelling at the sequence of events that first brought me there and then, three or four years later, made me the owner of the place. It might so easily never have happened; I might have missed all the joy that has come to me from those fifty acres of rough ground. Sometimes I cannot believe that it was an accident; sometimes I feel sure that God always intended me to be a landowner; sometimes I fancy that, from all eternity, he has been planning High Park as the place that would some day turn into my little portion of heaven upon earth.

Sitting by the sike the other day, and marvelling all over again at the fact that the fields all round me were mine, sitting there and drifting between hope and memory and present contentment, sitting there with vague schemes of improvement, with pleasant memories

of past seasons and with the immediate delight of the sights on every side of me, sitting there quietly and smoking, I felt – as I so often feel – all the power of the hold that High Park has taken on my heart in the course of the last ten years. And my inability to get you round fifty acres of land without stopping every few minutes to sit and smoke or stand and stare, without turning aside into a stream of memory and association and reflection, this incapacity of mine has helped me to realise all over again why I so love the place.

It is beyond doubt very beautiful, but there is so much more than beauty there; for I can never look at any part of it without seeing much more than my eyes are showing me; always there is some recollection from last winter or from five seasons ago, perhaps even from last week; and I walk every inch of it with plans for the future as well as with these memories from the past. Next year there are spruces and larches to plant on either side of the new pen; there will be Scots pines too for the strip that runs along the top of Middle Pasture; and the ditch that runs down its west side must sooner or later be fenced off and planted up and turned into another little drive.

At High Park, just as on the rivers that I have fished for so many years, there is a richness of association that I find nowhere else, not even in places that I have known much longer or in places where I spend more time. High Park is very special because I own it and am thus free to shape and change and to involve myself more deeply, more powerfully in its earth and in its landscape; but it seems to me, more generally, that a sportsman's places, which seep out moods and images and memories, become in a very special way a part of himself, and continually they are enriching both themselves and the man who loves them with the growing deposit of experience. It is like the accumulation of leaf-mould beneath the trees. It is like this on the Eden and the Wharfe as well as at High Park. And in these places, in these sacred little corners of the world, we find a blend and an intensity of feelings that belongs to them

alone; we find excitement and peace at the same time; often we feel a deep and thankful contentment; sometimes we are lost in praise; there are times when our pleasure in these places is exuberant; there are calmer and more thoughtful times. We share these places with our friends; we spend long hours in them by ourselves. They are the places where we go to disentangle ourselves from the clutter of our surrounding lives; we go to them to free and to find ourselves and we do this in the name of sport; but what we call sport is properly a sort of ritual of praise, a sort of reverent acknowledgment of the sustaining beauty and all the richness of the created world.

If, by the way, these thoughts seem to you to be windy and empty or tedious thoughts, then you will loathe this book, for it will be full of thoughts along similar lines, though there will be dogs in between, dogs and pheasants and ducks and rabbits and probably a few woodcock. There will be late summer at High Park, followed by the autumn and the winter and the sport that belongs to them. I have done a very poor job of introducing you to my little kingdom; you will get to know it much better in the months ahead, and some of you may know something of it already from earlier books and from my articles in *Shooting Times*. Meanwhile I had better attempt to introduce myself, although it is again possible that you may already have met me in earlier writings either as a trout fisher or as a shooting man.

If you have met the fisher you will know that he is not of the sort who fills his bag whenever he goes to the river, the sort who casts with unerring precision and delicacy, who sees and identifies the fly on the water, selects an appropriate and beautifully tied artificial from one of his well-ordered boxes, flicks it over the nose of an unsuspecting two-pounder, promptly brings up the two-pounder and then calmly drives home the hook, playing the trout thus attached to his line with an unruffled judgment and with a perfect application of pressure, until it admits that it has met its master, turns on its side

and is drawn smoothly over the net. There are days when I return from the river feeling moderately pleased with myself; there are just as many days when I creep home with an empty bag; after losing the only trout I hooked because I caught my rod in an overhanging branch; after putting down fish after fish with bungled casts or a thoughtless choice of fly; after spending more time rescuing my flies from alders and willows than putting them onto the water; after failing to cope with a downstream wind; after falling in twice and tearing my waders on a rusty strand of barbed wire; after fishing, in short, like a man who has learned nothing since the day forty years ago when he first held a fly rod in his hand.

I am not an expert fisher and I am most certainly not an expert shot. My experience as a shooting man, moreover, is limited. Over the years I have done a bit of wildfowling, but only with small rewards and I confess that, in general, I found it cold and uncomfortable. I have never shot a goose, although I can remember the end of an inland flight when the moonlight was suddenly filled with honking; and then a skein of Canadas came low over the pond where we were crouching in the hope of a last duck or two. Geese can never have offered a shooter an easier target, but my surprise and excitement got the better of me and I went home at the end of it all with only a brace of mallard to hang in the shed where my game waits until it is time for me to get it ready for the freezer or the table.

Many of you will have killed more pigeon in a single day than I have managed in more than thirty years. My experience of partridges is small and I have no experience at all of shooting abroad. I love sitting in a grouse butt; unfortunately I do it so infrequently that, on those rare and grand occasions when I find myself peering out expectantly over the heather, I also find that I can hit very few of the birds that some instinct for self-preservation sends skimming over the heather in the direction of my gun. I am much

more likely to shoot a duck as it flights into a grey pond on the edge of the darkness, but the ponds where I sit waiting for them, with old Merlin at my side, rarely bring in more than a dozen or so mallard and sometimes a few teal. Whenever I leave one of my ponds with as many as four duck in the bag I feel very happy indeed; and, incidentally, I think that flighting duck, although I do it on a very modest scale, is perhaps my favourite form of sport with the gun.

I suppose I kill twenty or thirty rabbits in the course of an average year. I probably miss as many as I kill, which is a pity because the taste of rabbit-flesh is something of which I never grow weary (it is, by the way, the perfect accompaniment for the subtle delights of Chinon from a good year). Most winters bring at least a handful of woodcock to my gun (only burgundy will do for woodcock, and it should be the best in your cellar); some winters bring a few snipe (burgundy again), but most shooting days are pheasant days, spent at High Park or on the land rented by my syndicate near Settle, with perhaps three or four guest days on somewhat grander shoots. My own days are small days and it is a very rare day that discharges more than twenty cartridges from my gun; if half of those twenty shots bring a pheasant falling from the sky, I return home convinced that I am a mighty sportsman, and usually then I uncork something special to turn my dinner into a celebration; something special almost certainly means claret since, at the end of pheasant-days, I like to honour my quarry by eating it and by toasting both the splendour of its flight and the subtle richness of its flesh. It will, of course, be a pheasant from an earlier shoot: one that has hung in the shed for a week or ten days before being turned into food.

Occasionally I take a little practice with clay birds, but it has yet to teach me why, on some days in the field, I can hit pheasants with a fair degree of confidence, even high and curling ones, whereas on other days even undemanding birds fly on their way

without a care in the world, serenely unaware that the recent sound of gunfire was, in the mind of the man standing below them with the gun, intended to be accompanied by their sudden descent from the sky. I should like to claim that I am an instinctive shot; but your instinctive shot is properly one whose instinct gets it consistently right. The truth is that I am something much less impressive; I am your inconsistent, your plain average shot, and there you more or less have it.

You will not, if you come shooting with me in this book, read of exploits to set beside those of Lords Ripon and Walsingham. There will be very few right-and-lefts (is this the correct from of the plural?) and you are unlikely to count up dead pheasants in hundreds at the end of a day's sport. You will join a few friends, sitting under a hedge at midday, chewing a few sandwiches and pies, drinking a tot of whisky and discussing how a lunchtime bag of six birds can somehow be made to reach double figures in the course of the afternoon.

As well as my human friends you will often meet two dogs. They are both springers and one of them is the apple of his master's eye. He is liver and white, big and long-backed, and at nine he is just beginning to show the first signs of age and stiffness. He is called Merlin and I have already mentioned him. He was fully trained when I bought him just under eight years ago and he is rather less than half trained now. He runs into shot, though usually only if the shot has found its target; sometimes he sets off in pursuit of a particularly tempting rabbit, and he often pegs pheasants that are slow to get onto the wing; but still, in spite of his years, he hunts all day and is eager for more at the end of it all; gorse is his speciality, and the thicker and sharper it is the more he likes it, plunging in wildly to flush out any pheasants that have gone on retreat into its darkest and densest corners. He is a great hunter, a great retriever and, as long as he has a lead round his neck, an exemplary peg dog.

Digger is the second of my spaniels, three years younger than Merlin, black and white with ears already greying. He is not a model spaniel and, though his name is Digger – more properly Digby – I often curse him as the Prince of Darkness or the Hound of Hell, especially when he disappears into the gorse and, deaf to the roaring of my voice and the shrieking of my whistle, starts flushing birds hundreds of yards away from the guns. There are times when I feel sure that I hate him and he never goes with me to other men's shoots.

You will meet my friends' dogs too, with their many virtues and their occasional failings; you will meet the boys who help me at High Park. They will be planting trees or mending pheasant pens or dragging sacks of wheat to inaccessible hoppers while I sit smoking down by the sike; sometimes they will be shooting with me as a reward for their help; they will probably be shooting straighter than their host. You will not, by the way, be expected to spend any time in my classroom and I promise never to start holding forth about my life as a schoolmaster. Three or four boys who love shooting will be virtually the only reminder that the author of this book earns his daily crust in front of a blackboard.

I cannot think of anything else to say as an introduction to the themes and the characters of this book, except perhaps to claim in its recommendation that it is very unlikely to make you feel jealous. If you read what follows you will almost certainly be able to tell yourself that you enjoy better sport than I do, and that you are a better amateur keeper, a better shot and a better dog-handler than at least one person in the world. I shall, of course, be very happy to receive letters of advice and sympathy, or even invitations to shoot famous marshes, coverts or moors. If you have read this book, then you will, at least, know more or less what to expect when I turn up.

CHAPTER TWO

AUGUST

Releasing poults; the first fortnight; August
dreams and nightmares; leisurely summer
duties; feather pecking; thoughts about
hunting and the power of Mr Average

My shooting year starts in August. It does not start on the Glorious
Twelfth, with me sitting somewhere high in the Pennine sunshine,
sitting or leaning there with the contents of a box of cartridges laid
out for easy access on the turf top of my butt, waiting there with my
gun still broken and placed next to that line of neatly paired
cartridges, sitting there in a hum of summer flies and waiting in that
distinctive mood of nervous expectation that comes to all occasional
grouse shooters at such times, sitting and waiting and surrounded by
heather while, a long way in front of me, the drive is prepared and
energetic young beaters and arthritic old flankers find their positions
on the moor and then, with insistent bawling from the keepers to
hold the line or move forward on the left or slow down on the right,
they begin their advance towards the butts.

It may be that, some time in August, I *shall* form part of such a

scene, but it will not be the start of my shooting year, which happens on the first of the month – or as near to it as the weather allows – with the arrival at High Park of one hundred and fifty pheasant poults. Much has already been done to prepare for their coming; food and water have been brought to the pens; wire has been checked and patched; the electric fences have been put in working order; drinkers and hoppers have been cleaned and filled. There will also have been jobs to do in earlier months of the year; gorse will have been hacked; trees will have been planted, new cover will have been cut and new fences may have excluded the sheep from another acre or two of my land. The arrival of my poults is not the beginning of my work; but it is an important occasion and it seems like a new beginning, seems like the start of my shooting year.

I buy my poults at eight weeks old and I have their flight feathers pulled. There is a reason for both the advanced age of my poults and their temporary inability to fly. In July, as soon as term ends, I spend a week or more trying to catch trout; then I head North and spend a fortnight staggering up and down Scottish mountains, raising my stick at any grouse that flush from the heather and invariably concluding that my aim was true. July is my holiday month. In August I devote myself to one hundred and fifty pheasant poults. I buy them at eight weeks – rather than the more usual six – because the beginning of August is a little late for release if you want your birds ready by early November. If you are buying only one hundred and fifty poults, the additional expense scarcely matters; you can justify it, anyway, by telling yourself that older birds are somewhat less likely to fall sick in the release pens; I also tell myself that I only have a month or five weeks for the main business of release; once term starts I can no longer be at High Park every day. But if all goes well and if, by the beginning of school, there are still almost one hundred and fifty pheasant poults in the vicinity of my pens, they will by then be thirteen weeks old and at least half capable of looking after themselves; and so I can open up the pens, if they are not already open; I can wish my poults well and, unless disaster strikes, which will almost certainly be in the shape of a fox, I can come out to check on their progress, to move and to fill hoppers and to harass crows, just two or three times a week. Disaster has passed me by in the last three or four seasons and I hope to God it will spare me again this year.

The smallness of my shoot is the reason for the pulled flight-feathers. I want my birds in the pens for their first three weeks at High Park, not fluttering over the wire and then hopping over my boundaries the day after their arrival. I want them to settle down, to grow used to their pens, learning to think of them as home and perhaps even falling half in love with them. The problem with this prolonged confinement is that it encourages feather-pecking, but the pens are big enough for it to remain a minor problem. I think the pulled flight-feathers are a good idea.

My pheasants go into two pens, ninety into the older and bigger one, which is about ninety yards round, and sixty into the new pen (roughly fifty yards in circumference). The new pen was built only last year. I was the designer; I also did some digging with a spade and drove in a few posts with vigorous blows from a fencing mallet, but most of the labour was done by three schoolboys, while the designer sat smoking on a stile, issuing orders and offering invaluable advice. Until the new pen turned from a good idea into a grand fabric of timber and wire, one hundred and thirty five poults went into the one pen. Feather-pecking was undoubtedly worse in the old days; a second advantage of the new pen is that it helps to spread birds more evenly over the shoot. I do not, by the way, bother with pop-holes. There are two of them in the old pen, constructed in accordance with the specifications of the Game Conservancy, but I blocked them off years ago; my pheasants never seemed to pick up the knack of popping through them back to safety. They seemed a pointless risk and so they were wired up and have never since been opened. Facing

the main gate of the old pen there is a smaller gate at ground level. I walk – or chase – my birds back out of danger through these two gates (and through the single gate in the smaller new pen).

There comes a time when pheasant poults no longer know what is good for them. As the days pass they roost higher in the trees within their pens; more and more of them, as each successive dawn brings them down from roost, reach earth on the wrong side of the wire; and it soon becomes impossible to persuade more than a portion of them to scamper back to safety through the gates. They insist, in ever increasing numbers, on staying out both all day and all night. Every year, when this happens, I have to remind myself that my pens are, in fact, release pens and not permanent aviaries, although I still keep them closed as long as possible, hoping to protect those unadventurous and sensible birds that prefer to remain inside. But the urge for freedom is as infectious as gapes and, once the exodus has really started, it is not long before only a few birds are left inside the pens. Now is the time – usually early in September – to throw caution to the winds, to open all the gates and a few gaps in the wire, declaring the release more or less over for the year and commending my birds to the intercession of every sympathetic saint whose name I can remember. Then I go round propping open gates, snipping away with my wire cutters and turning off the electric fences that have helped me to sleep at night for the last four weeks. It always seems a reckless performance; I postpone it from day to day, but the time comes when it can be put off no longer and so at last it is done.

For their first fortnight in the pens my poults feast on turkey grower pellets; they are cheaper than pheasant growers, they can be bought without some ridiculous certificate from a vet and they seem just as full of prophylactic medications. My poults, at any rate, seem perfectly happy with pellets made for turkeys. After about a fortnight I begin to feed wheat. I do not start, as many do, by mixing it with the pellets, for, in my experience, this produces mounds of grain beneath the hoppers, with pheasants searching through them for the richer and softer food they have learned to love. I scatter wheat thinly round the pens for a few days. The poults peck at it disdainfully. Then I put it into my feeding trays, then in the ground hoppers, then I fill up the hanging slit-hoppers with wheat as they become empty. It seems to work and by the beginning of September the move to grain should have been more or less accomplished. I put out piles of grit as soon as I start encouraging my poults to sample the austere delights of corn.

Except in the first weeks of release there is no hand feeding at High Park. There are hoppers in the pens and there are hoppers all over the place. Once they are all up there are about thirty of them and, once the birds are out of the pens, it is the hoppers that must hold them on my ground. Most of my hoppers, until they began a new life with holes or slits in their bottom ends, were five-gallon detergent containers. Three or four are much bigger, stand on their own legs and, long before they were filled with grain, were full of mango chutney instead. I could do with more of them. They go in places that are difficult to reach when the autumn rains have limited the range of my Land Rover. This season, as the shooting draws nearer, I plan to move more and more hoppers towards the centre of my little kingdom. I shall explain the reasons for this when I begin to do it, though they are, I suppose, fairly obvious.

There is nothing original in my method of releasing pheasants. I learned most of it from men who know ten times as much as I do about the whole business, and I do not pretend to myself that I have made important advances in the theory and practice of poult management. But amateur keepers are always interested in the way another man does things and, anyway, if you are going to read about a season's shooting at High Park, it seems appropriate to me that you should know something of the process that leads up to it. It lasts

for three months and is therefore almost exactly as long as the shooting itself, which never starts properly before November and finishes, oddly but pleasingly, on the first of February.

In August I spend my days looking after young pheasants and my nights dreaming about them. Now dreams, it seems to me, are of very limited interest to anyone but the people who dream them; those who describe their dreams to others are usually crashing bores. It is a form of self-expression that is not much of a temptation for me, because I can very rarely remember my dreams, and the confused strands of them that survive the night are most certainly poor material for general knowledge. I imagine that my best dreams concern themselves with claret, with tastings (and gifts) of Margaux and Latour and Mouton Rothschild in their greatest vintages. It is probable too that I catch three-pound trout from rivers of wine, casting a Tup's Indispensable onto pools full of Leoville Barton '70, and perhaps, in between the three-pounders, I pick up my gun, which just happens to be lying conveniently on the riverbank, in order to bring high pheasants, which just happen to be flying overhead at convenient moments, tumbling into the stream. Merlin, of course, will retrieve them in exemplary fashion, pausing for just a second on the edge of the stream to sniff the refined and complex bouquet of the flowing liquid.

I think my happy dreams are something of this sort. Recurring nightmares – and I can manage to recall one or two of them – find me locked up for the weekend with two dozen public school headmasters, or condemned to share a candlelit dinner with Tony and Cherie Blair. But things are different in August, for in August my pheasants come to High Park and, in August, my good and my bad dreams are filled neither with wine nor with headmasters nor with prime ministers. Those of you who release pheasant poults doubtless dream similar dreams yourselves; so you can take this as an opportunity to compare notes.

My dreams in August are full of pheasant pens, and the fragrance of claret is replaced by the stink of Renardine. It is always deep night and, in the good dreams, my pheasants are sleeping serenely within their fortresses. Foxes appear from time to time: sometimes, catching the strange and repellent smell that loads the night air, they turn tail and run away with barely a glance at the slumbering forms inside my pens; at other times they refuse to be deterred so easily, approaching more closely until, with jaws already slavering, they press their predatory snouts onto a strand of electrified wire, promptly leap ten feet into the air before racing off to tell their friends that there is painful magic at work round Catlow's pheasant pens and that in future they must be avoided. Down by the sike, meanwhile, a hungry mink, drawn by the irresistible fragrance of rotting tunny flesh, is sliding into one of my traps, where I shall find it hissing and spitting in the morning and feel that I have done the wild life of Britain, as well as my pheasant poults, a good turn by killing it.

Foxes rebound from the electric fence, mink cannot wait to imprison themselves in my cage-traps; now and then the silence of the night is broken as a cunningly sited fen-trap snaps the neck of a stoat too inquisitive for its continued survival. A poult or two opens an eye at the sound, wonders drowsily what woke him up and almost immediately falls fast asleep again. Perhaps an owl floats over the pen, but he dislikes the blinking lights on top of the posts and floats away with a silent flap of his wings.

Meanwhile my pheasants snore contentedly through the night, their heads full of dreams very different from those of their keeper: dreams of hot and sunny days, days full of water and pellets, of dust baths and easy living, with no ghost of a threat from the host of dangers that surround young pheasants on every side in the wild world beyond the protection of their pens.

Things are less satisfactory in my August nightmares. To begin with I have forgotten to turn on the electric fences, and so whole armies of foxes treat jumping over them this way and that as a ritual preliminary to a night of delightful slaughter. After this light-hearted prelude they dig under the wire, unless they stream into the pen through the gate that I have considerately left open for them. Then they devote themselves wholeheartedly to their favourite hobby of tearing off heads. A few pheasants escape the jaws of the foxes, flapping over the wire with their heads still intact. But here the mink, mink with no fondness for tunny-baited traps, mink that insist on the raw flesh of game for their midnight feasts, here the sharp-fanged mink are waiting for them in murderous silence, while stoats are lined up three deep behind them, ready to pounce if any of my birds flutter through the darkness unplundered by the ravenous mink. There is, of course, a brown owl sitting and blinking in every tree, wondering when it will be his turn to join in the fun. And just in case any of my poults manage to make it through the night, all the sparrow hawks of Cumbria are dreaming the same dream, which is concerned with pheasant flesh and its easy availability round the pens of High Park Farm.

It is no wonder that sometimes I wake early in August and thunder out unshaven to the farm just as fast as the old Land Rover will get me there, convinced that I shall find both my pens still running with blood and the land all round them littered with torn fragments of pheasant. I am delighted to report that, so far this August, I have discovered no scenes of recent carnage. I have found the dismembered remains of one poult and am inclined to put the blame on an owl. I have picked another poult dead from one of the drinkers and cannot think how he met his end. A third poult has managed to choke herself on a length of baling twine, and the fault here, of course, is all mine for so carelessly leaving dangerous litter inside the pen. But the rest of them show no signs of disease or stress; they are eating and drinking as healthy pheasant poults

should and they are looking bigger every day. There is still time for disaster in many forms, but my birds have already been with me for three weeks and I am now daring to hope that all will be well.

It is the last day of August and I have just said farewell to my pheasants for three days. I am off to the Wharfe in search of a few trout, leaving the birds in the expert care of my friend Austin. It will be good to think of fishing again rather than of pheasants; it is almost a month since my hand last held a fishing rod and it has been too long a separation from rivers and the deep satisfactions that belong to them. I could, of course, make time for plenty of fishing in August. It does not take the whole of the day to feed and water one hundred and fifty pheasant poults; there are men who do it in an hour at the end of a day's work, or in even less time before the beginning of one; there are men, moreover, who do this for six or seven hundred, or even for a thousand birds. I could easily go fishing every day in August; and most years I do spend a few August afternoons or evenings on the Eden, but there is never quite the same sense of dedication that fills my fishing at other times of the year.

This is because I think of August as pheasant-time, as the month of the year when I belong almost entirely to High Park. It is a month set apart for me to spend as much time as possible on the little patch of land that is all my own, learning to love it more with each year that passes, doing what needs to be done and then wandering all over my fifty acres and discovering new beauty wherever I go. This afternoon, as I sat above the old pen and watched birds sitting and sunning and dusting themselves on the bank below me, some of them already with long tails, many of the cocks showing the first signs of their mature splendour, with the hoppers full of wheat and with a few birds pecking away beneath them, with the sun warm and golden on the bank and probing through the trees and glowing on the first blackberries – I thought this afternoon, as I sat above the pen and then walked down Pheasant Hill on my way to the Land Rover, what a delightful time the last month has been for me.

It must be very different for proper keepers; their pheasant time lasts all year, whereas mine lasts only a month and arrives each August as a welcome change. They are responsible for thousands of birds, while I have only one hundred and fifty in my care. Their livelihood, moreover, depends upon their keepering, and they must answer to their employer for how effectively it is done. As far as my pheasants are concerned I am my own master; recurring disasters in the pens would bring down only my own rather than another man's anger upon my head, and they would not fill me with the fear of poverty or force me to renounce claret in an effort to make ends meet.

As long as things are going well, and unless I have been visited by one of my pheasant-time nightmares, I take a leisurely approach to my duties as the keeper of my own birds. I do not rush out to High Park at first light; the alarm clock wakes me up at eight o'clock and I lie in bed, drinking tea and listening to John

Humphrys being rude to his victims on Radio Four. Nine o'clock means that it is time to get up, time to shave and dress and let the dogs out; then there is breakfast (usually kippers or scrambled eggs), which is followed by the first tobacco of the day; then I climb into the Land Rover and drive off to my work.

It is with just a hint of apprehension that I walk up to the pens, especially on the first few mornings after the birds have arrived. Once I know that the night has passed without slaughter, once I have discovered that my pheasants have not all turned into headless corpses and are not all staggering round the pens in the grip of some sudden plague that will see the lot of them dead before noon; once, in short, I have found them spared for another day, then I settle down happily to my tasks: walking birds back into the pens, filling hoppers and drinkers, carrying sacks of pellets or wheat up from their shed by the meadow gate, heaving containers of water up from the sike. Then there are the traps to check, and to reset if they have claimed any victims in the course of the night (four mink and a single stoat so far this pheasant-time). There will be more hoppers to hang, back in the wood or down in the larches or up above the gorse on the other side of the sike. And as each day passes my hope grows: my hope that most of the poults will survive to maturity and fly over the guns on one of those windy days in November, or on a bright and frosty day before Christmas or, best of all, on those hard, cold days when the air really bites in the first weeks of the New Year.

To return to the delights of my August pheasant-time, once I have fed and watered my birds and wandered here and there, busying myself with this and that or with nothing in particular, it will be time for a long smoke, for a cup of tea from my flask and for a pie or a sandwich. Unless rain forces me to seek shelter in the Land Rover, the setting for my lunch will be the bank above the old pen or the stile near the new one, where I eat and drink and watch

my birds, telling myself how well they are doing and taking at least some of the credit for their keeper.

There has been some feather-pecking in the last weeks, but it has not been serious; there have been no bleeding rumps and, now that most of the birds are out of the pens, it is already almost a thing of the past. For the first time this year I have had gapes among my birds. I heard the first choking sounds of it about a week ago; I treated the food in and round the pens with some magical lotion recommended by the vet (I think it is a dilute form of a medicine to treat worms in cattle). Whatever it is, the lotion has done its stuff; today I heard only one bird coughing and saw no twitching heads at all.

It is a good idea to spend some time just watching and listening; you may see and hear things that would otherwise pass unnoticed. This year I have amused myself by throwing twigs at two long-spurred cocks that have appeared round the old pen and rediscovered their taste for turkey pellets and easy pickings. As I watch and listen and throw twigs, I also have time to sit and think. My thoughts this pheasant time have been much concerned with the recent vote in the Commons to ban hunting with hounds; they are thoughts that have also followed me round in my active periods, asking me how long hunting is likely to survive and whether I believe that my activities at High Park, and along the margins of rivers, will some day be declared a criminal offence.

I have decided, in the course of several days' reflection, that hunting is probably doomed, that shooting may be seriously threat-ened within a generation and that fishing is safe for at least a century to come. I have also decided that the moral nonsense of this prospect means that it is almost certain to come true, and I do not believe that anything I or any one else chooses to write in defence of hunting will make it possible for men and women to follow

hounds for one more week of their lives or even for a single day. These are gloomy conclusions and, since the thoughts that lie behind them have been very much a part of this year's pheasant time, I shall now briefly set them forth.

A friend recently complained to me that the 'antis', his word for the activists among those opposed to fieldsports, were likely to gain their objectives within his own lifetime by putting an end to his three favourite recreations. He was not fond of the antis and I agreed with him that, as a class, they were unlovable creatures, but I insisted that he was wrong in thinking that such men threatened our sports in any serious fashion. I admitted that, if a group of them turned up in my apologies for coverts at the start of a shooting day, I should be disinclined to offer them a glass of dry sherry or a swig of sloe gin, but at the same time I maintained that, although they might on occasions disrupt our pleasure and make a damned nuisance of themselves, the end of hunting and shooting would never be brought about by their activities. I denied that these activities had played any part in moving public opinion against the pursuit of the fox; I even suggested to my friend that his antis might turn out to be good for him, arguing that the British distaste for extremists is always likely to prejudice the ordinary man against the causes which they champion with such intemperate fervour.

While feeding or watching my pheasants this month and while drinking my evening half-bottle of claret, or while sipping my single large whisky before saying my prayers and going to bed, I have sometimes wondered whether this last point was really justified; but I have not changed in my conviction that the future of fieldsports will be decided, not by the actions and beliefs of a few passionate men, but by the thoughts and feelings of Mr Average, whoever he might be; for it is Mr Average, whoever he is and wherever he lives (which is surely somewhere remote from the life of the country-side), it is Mr Average whose opinions are certain to prevail in the

long run. And Mr Average is in the ascendant; he is much more powerful, and much more dangerous, than he was even ten years ago, which is because prime ministers and politicians are suddenly less inclined to argue with him; they are much more eager to predict his opinions than to shape or to change them. Very few of them are willing to defy him on a matter of deep conviction. Almost none of them are willing to point out to him that his thinking on a particular issue is ill-informed and incoherent. They are much more likely to praise his instinctive wisdom and his sound common sense.

Before deciding to try my hand at political commentary I was suggesting that, although Mr Average – I use the title, by the way, for the sake of convenience and without a sneer – I was suggesting that although Mr Average may be influenced by zealots and idealists, his response to their activities is very difficult to predict. He is certainly swayed by what he sees on television and what he reads in The Sun. Once his opinion on something takes shape it usually sets firm. There is a sclerotic tendency to his thought that makes Mr Average, mentally speaking, a difficult man to budge. But there are certain times when the rigidity of his thinking softens to the influence of currents of change; there are times of slow, almost unconscious ferment when his view on a given matter very gradually reshapes itself.

Such a time, I think, has come to him in his attitude to field-sports; the reshaping, in fact, is almost over; the time is almost past when it will be possible to change the set of his mind, for the crust has already formed and very soon everything beneath the crust will be as solid as concrete; any modification of Mr Average's mind will then be effectively impossible for decades to come.

It is very important to remember that Mr Average's attitude to fishing, about which he probably knows a little and may even know a lot, is very different from his attitude to shooting, about which he

is unlikely to know very much at all. He knows nothing about hunting, and this is very unfortunate for those who hunt, because Mr Average is at his stubbornest when his opinions are based on ignorance or falsehood.

Fishermen have nothing to fear from Mr Average, who may even be a fisherman himself; if he is not, then perhaps his neighbour spends part of his weekends with a fishing rod in his hands; and the knowledge that Ted next door loves catching roach and does not celebrate a successful day by drinking human blood or sacrificing babies beneath the light of the new moon, this knowledge means that Mr Average looks with an indulgent eye upon fishing as the blameless occupation of ordinary men. Fishing is normal; ordinary people do it and Mr Average is disposed to approve of whatever he regards as normal and ordinary.

He is not, moreover, inclined to feel much sympathy for fish. They do not fill him with tender thoughts, as do the ducks on the park pond with their little ducklings squeaking round them so affectingly, or the robin in his garden that sits so confidingly on the handle of his spade, or those innocent fox cubs that he sees on television, romping in front of their den and playing so amusingly with the bones of a dead pheasant.

Mr Average knows from experience that fishermen are decent and ordinary folk; the thought of fish on the end of fishing lines with hooks in their mouths does not fill him with a sense of moral outrage. We fishers, moreover, have promoted our sport very cleverly as the contemplative man's recreation, as a sort of idyll along the margins of quiet water, a form of active reflection that helps weary souls to win back God's best gift of peace. Taken together, all this means that Mr Average does not associate fishing with the suffering and death of animals. He associates it with Ted next door and on the whole he approves.

When he thinks of shooting Mr Average is much less likely to smile. He does not shoot, nor does his neighbour, and Mr Average probably thinks that shotguns are designed to make pheasants and grouse impossible to miss. It is very unfortunate that guns are a necessary part of the sport of shooting; they are very different from roach poles and fly rods; they are dangerous, they make loud noises and bad men use them to slaughter their own kind. You cannot really blame Mr Average for regarding guns and those who own them with dark suspicion. And he knows that shooting men use guns to kill birds, and he wonders what pleasure they can possibly derive from the killing. Mr Average watches television and he loves nature programmes; he loves the pheasants that strut so splendidly across his screen and the raptors that fly across it with such predatory grace; and he has heard – and he has, by the way, heard the truth – that gamekeepers have been known to poison hawks and falcons and harriers, so that rich men can murder a few more grouse than would have fallen to their guns if those hawks and falcons had been left to fly.

For years and years Mr Average scarcely thought about shooting. He was dimly aware that it was something country squires and noble lords got up to. In those days Mr Average was inclined to respect the gentry and the aristocracy; at any rate it never occurred to him that he had any right to interfere with their recreations. He was undismayed by the annual feature on the television news that showed the prime minister of the day setting out to make the most of the Glorious Twelfth. He is less tolerant now. He has more or less made up his mind that shooting birds for sport is wrong; his mind is setting and we have very little time to reshape the mould.

His views on hunting are, I fear, beyond reform. Remember that his ignorance is total and expect him to be at his most intractable. Mr Average thinks that men and women who chase foxes are savages who delight in torture and the spectacle of blood, primitive aristocrats and degenerate backwoodsmen who have never advanced out of the barbarity that was general until very recent and more enlightened times. Mr Average thinks that hunting is an anachronism and that now is the time to get rid of it. He is likely to vote for those who claim to agree with him, and I suspect that he cannot be moved. It will take something like a miracle to persuade Mr Average that hunting people are often ordinary human beings who love their wives and their children and are, in fact, full of admiration for foxes. Those who hunt will try to work this little miracle. I do not envy them but I wish them well and I shall feel very angry indeed on the day that hunting with hounds is finally banned.

I think I have said enough about Mr Average. I think it is time to forget about the future of fieldsports for a few pages, time to return to August at High Park. It is true that, while busy among my

birds this August, I have thought at length about the common man's view of country sports; it is also true that my conclusions have not filled me with confidence for the immediate prospect for hunting and the long-term future for shooting. I have done much of my thinking at lunch time, sitting by one of the pens and eating a sandwich or two, then filling my mug with tea and lighting my pipe and seeing where my thoughts take me. Eventually they always lead me to the conclusion that it is time to stand up and start getting on with things.

After lunch I often saunter back through the wood to see how much new growth is springing up in the clearings that my chain-saw made for me in the spring (the sheep prevent much regeneration, though the felled timber and brash provide good cover for my birds). Then the flight-pond needs feeding and, of course, the dogs need a run, with some attempt to prepare them for the work that lies ahead; and there is always the hope that Digger will suddenly turn into a model gun dog, confounding my guests with his exemplary behaviour when they come to shoot at High Park later in the year.

This August my war against crows has been a sad tale of defeat. On half a dozen afternoons I have lurked in ambush, carefully concealed near one of the groups of hoppers which they regularly attack; but always they have decided to mob the hoppers where there is no one waiting for their arrival with a loaded gun. Sooner or later I shall catch up with them; I shall hang black corpses from the trees as a warning to their surviving friends and relatives that death waits for them in the vicinity of my feeders. I never, by the way, try to shoot crows once the pheasant shooting has started; pheasants in season should hear gunfire as rarely as possible, especially on a miniature shoot like mine; but, until they begin to associate loud bangs with danger, you can let off your gun just as often as you choose without frightening a single pheasant from your ground. Even the old cocks scratching round the pens seem to have forgotten that in January the sound of a gun was for them the signal for immediate departure over, or more often under, the nearest boundary fence. Perhaps they think that turkey pellets and easy pickings are worth the risk.

It is good, as the month advances, to see how the blackberries are beginning to deserve their name; it is good to eat a few of the blackest and juiciest berries for your afternoon tea. Mushrooms are appearing in the pastures and some of them usually go home with me to be added to the evening's stew. Rowans have been red for weeks now and the haws too are reddening. All day long the wires over the meadow are full of swallows, and every day the heavy green of summer trees lightens a little as more leaves begin to wrinkle and fade. There are dry and crumpled leaves floating down the sike now and the ground beneath the birches is scattered with splashes of umber and yellow.

Pheasant time brings restless days when the wind blows and moans beneath the cloud. There are dark and still days beneath a sullen sky. There are days when the wind chases white clouds through the sky, when the willows stream silver, when the aspens quiver in every leaf and the world seems to have regained something of its spring freshness. I am out in all such days and I like the lot of them. I am out in the wet ones too, which bring their own pleasures; you can listen to the sound of the rain falling on the leaves; you can watch the drops slowly forming and swelling on the leaf-tips and the leaning rushes; you can look forward to rain-freshened rivers for your September trouting.

But always in August, especially late in August, there come a few days of the sort that I associate with August alone. They are days that reach their fullness in the late afternoon, for the breeze has died away by then; and the light has turned gold. Long yellow stalks hang feathered and dry; the morning drift of thistledown has settled

on the gorse and the grass and the berried brambles. Somewhere in the trees a robin whistles its late-summer song; finches and tits make small sounds through the branches; pheasants rub themselves sleepily in the dust and, down there at the foot of the hill, the sike murmurs over the mossy stones.

The sun shines; the leaves are still; gorse pods pop in the heat. With my work ended, I am probably lying at my ease, with two spaniels lying somewhere beside me, lying up there in the mottled shade on Pheasant Hill, drowsy from the warm air and the day's moderate exertions, drowsy and content and disinclined to stir myself for another ten minutes or perhaps for half an hour; and sometimes, as I lounge back in the grass, sometimes it seems that time, like me, has lolled its head and closed its eyes, that the season has surrendered to its own influence and lost any will to change or develop or move on; sometimes it seems that I shall lie for ever in this warm and sleepy world somewhere between summer and autumn, in a slowly fading world that will never fade away into something new. I tell myself dreamily that I release pheasants just for the pleasure of this present and sprawling contentment; for winter will never come with its short days and its sharp air and with the sport that belongs to them; September will never come, with its new school year and its last days on the river and its first evening flight. It will be late August for ever, warm and heavy-eyed and purposeless, and it will always be the afternoon.

The illusion is so compelling that I usually surrender to it by falling fast asleep. It is only on waking that I see how the shadows of the larches have edged a few inches up the hill towards me; and I feel how, even in the afternoon, the beginning of coolness is already creeping onto the air. I realise that, however things might have seemed to me half an hour ago, time is in fact still marching on. I tell myself that, since it now looks as though I shall have to earn my living in a classroom come September, I had better get back

to Sedbergh and get the dogs fed and look at my books for an hour or two. After that there will, of course, be half a bottle of claret (or burgundy) with my supper, and after supper I may tie a few flies. I think that, on the whole, I prefer a world in which time passes, but those afternoons in late August when it seems briefly to have lost the knack, those August afternoons are undoubtedly among the best afternoons of my annual pheasant-time.

CHAPTER THREE

SEPTEMBER

*Fishing the Wharfe; lust among the tups;
anxiety about my portrait; cartridges per
pheasant; war on crows; hopes at the start of
season; duck flighting; beauty of fishing and
shooting; a few words with the Prime Minister*

I spent the first five days of the month fishing in Wharfedale. I caught twenty six trout and killed fourteen of them, which are now in the deep freeze waiting their turn to be eaten. I like to be well-stored with trout at the season's end; their appearance on a plate in the middle of winter makes an excuse for Chablis; it also wakes memories of the spring and the summer, at the same time stirring pleasant longings for the coming of another spring with the beginning of another trout season.

The Wharfe was very low and it was much easier to frighten trout than to catch them. Every day was the same, with the fish feeding for hours on end on little black flies. The best pattern for them was unquestionably the Badger Black, tied on an eighteen hook. The dressing, if you are interested, is simplicity itself, with a

body of crow or magpie herl wound over purple silk which also forms the rib; the fly is then finished with two very short badger hackles, making a fly that is buoyant and easy to follow even in rough water. Other patterns caught me a few trout but the Badger Black accounted for more than half my total.

The weather had forgotten that it was September. There was no hint of frost in the mornings; there was no sudden chill on the evening air. All day long the sun shone with midsummer ferocity; every afternoon it turned stifling and close and, through it all, the river crept very wearily on its way. The weather was unseasonable but, in spite of the weather, there were signs of early autumn every-where. There were packs of full-grown mallard round every corner, rising from the river in twenties and thirties and turning my thoughts from trout-fishing to shooting duck, until I remembered that I cannot find a dealer anywhere in Cumbria with a single bismuth cartridge to sell me. It will probably be Christmas before Merlin and I first wait for the sound of wings on the edge of our little flight pond just over the boundary from High Park.

The parties of mallard told me that it was September, as did the tufted and ragged brown thistles in all the pastures. The warm air was thick with drifting down; the matted grass was full of crane flies; there were yellow keys hanging from the ashes and the sycamores; the leaves of the sycamores were mildewed and stained with black spots; and many of them were dry and shrivelled, while others were yellow and already floating down the pools. And, though there were swallows and martins talking restlessly up in the sky, there were no longer any swifts screaming above them; there were dippers and wagtails along the edges of the water, but there were no sandpipers flying low over the stream. Even the water was flowing with that autumnal tinge of brown: a tinge that comes from the moss and the weeds and all the growth that has been creeping over the riverbed – coating the rocks, choking the gravel, waving its

slimy strands in the current – all through the warm days of the summer, growth that is itself now feeling the influence of the season and turning to decay.

There were gatherings of tups in some of the pastures; they stood there in panting huddles and, provoked by the first stirrings of competitive lust, they grumbled and grunted at each other like emotionally disturbed diesel engines. The tups knew that it was September and that their time was approaching; the trout knew it as well for, though few of the fish I caught were soft and though none of them were ready to shed eggs or milt, many of them were already darkening, with a deeper yellow to the belly and a harder sheen to the black.

We fishers see signs of autumn all round us as we fish our rivers in September. It is these signs that make the atmosphere of our autumn fishing, giving it a feeling that is all its own: a feeling opposite and complementary to the feelings of those first trouting days way back in March and April; for then we fished with thoughts of the whole season ahead of us, impatient for warm breezes, for great hatches of fly and great falls of spinner and for huge rises of trout. Then the raw wind blew vigour into our lungs and we paced the cold banks with something of the happy restlessness that is the essence of the spring. In April we spent much of our time looking forwards; whereas in September I often lose myself in the past, for it is mostly in September that memories from earlier seasons come flocking under the leaves to take possession of the fishers who come there.

And so it is that, in September, as I sit by the side of Black Keld or Knipe Dub, I find myself drifting hazily between the present and the past, sometimes briefly uncertain whether I am a student in his early twenties or a balding schoolmaster who will be half a century old before Christmas.

Surrounding September fishing there is also all the sadness that belongs to the ending of things. The close of another season is now less than a month away, and all those memories come drifting down with the leaves, to float with them on the quiet currents of the river. We see an end approaching and we look away from it by looking back. There is something almost self-indulgent about the sadness of a fisher as he sits by a pool on a late afternoon in September, sunk in recollection and surrounded by all those signs of the fading year.

But, if a fisher is also a shooter, then September is for him a month of two moods; he is, in September at least, a man with a split personality; for though he sits by rivers and thinks quiet thoughts of the past as the leaves drift down and settle on his cap, he also strides out over the fields where he will soon be seeking sport with his gun. Here there is no place for the past; it is the future where your September shooter's heart is; and so, as he paces his boundaries, he encourages his poults to get on with it and grow longer tails; he urges his cock pheasants to strut in more mature and yet more gorgeous plumage; he tells his trees that it is high time they were shedding more leaves; and this year he may also be telling himself that, if only he had bought some of those new bismuth cartridges six months ago, before duck-shooters began queuing up in droves to get their hands on them, he would not still be waiting to shoot his first mallard of the season.

The very day after my return from Wharfedale I was out at High Park in the company of my friend Rod Calbrade, who had been sent there by the editor of *Shooting Times* with orders to take photographs. I spent most of the morning lurking behind trees in the hope of avoiding the camera's eye. In between times I looked at my birds and wished they were six weeks older. I showed Rod Beck Bank and The Rise and the little drives from the gorse; I took him through the wood and, down by the sike, we stood in those spots where the high birds come gliding over once the leaf is off the trees. It was the second week of September, but I felt none of the

September sadness that visits me by rivers. There was rather a sense of expectancy, with an eager looking forward to that day at the end of October when for the first time this season my pheasants will take to the sky in peril of their lives.

As a sportsman I lead, in September, a life of emotional extremes, and I thoroughly enjoy the contrast. I enjoy sitting on the banks of the Wharfe and surrendering to a stream of memories that takes me back almost to boyhood. But it is also good to go out to High Park and to forget the past, to walk my ground with no feelings of regret that September will soon be over, impatient rather to get through it as soon as possible on my way to winter pleasures. There are, by the way, feathers all over my flight pond; perhaps one of my friends will take pity on me and lend me a box of cartridges loaded with bismuth shot and suitable for an old English gun. I must get on the phone tonight.

I am now wishing that I had behaved differently when I went out to High Park a few days ago with Rod. You will remember me mentioning how I took cover behind trees as a means of escaping the merciless gaze of his lens. For my face, it seems to me, is of the sort that is better not made famous through the medium of photographic reproduction. Every tree on my land, every flower and blade of grass, every September pheasant scuttling through the rushes, every smallest feature of every field at High Park is ten times more worthy of such honour than are the rutted lines and the loose skin and the decaying teeth that form the prominent features of the portion of me that rises above the neck. The rest is hardly the stuff of lyric poetry, but the bit on top is undoubtedly the worst.

I am sure Rod caught me unawares and subsequently despatched to the editor of *Shooting Times* prints that revealed all the distinctive hideousness of my form; I suppose the editor and his staff have already spent hilarious coffee-breaks passing them from hand to hand and trying to decide which one of them is the most repulsive. Doubtless the editor himself immediately decided that none of them could ever appear in his magazine; unless he felt in the mood for a little black humour and, working on the assumption that no-one reads my column, decided to tuck away an image of its author in some corner of the page where it appears. Perhaps he has already indulged his taste for the grotesque; and, in spite of everything that I have just written, it is just such an error of judgement for which I am now praying; and, no! this is not because I have suddenly changed my mind and decided that I am strangely beautiful; it is rather that I have lost my hat and am longing to see a reminder of it, sitting on my head and tactfully shading the unlovely thing that lurks beneath it.

It was a hat of green cotton and it was already falling to bits when it first became mine. Now that it has gone I want to gaze at its image. I want to see again the line of dried sweat along the inner margin of the rim; I want to see the glint of the broken zip on the pocket beneath the crown, and to admire those gaping seams where the stitching had come loose. I want to see the loose band again and all those torn and hanging strands of cotton; I want to repossess, if only in a photograph, the shabby and floppy and faded greenness of my favourite and now missing hat.

It was given to me by a journalist who bought it years ago in Vietnam. I never asked Peter what adventures it had out in the East, although I suppose it found its life on top of me rather dull. Anyway it migrated to my head five summers ago and, except when my head has been indoors, it has rarely been off it since. It has climbed mountains in Scotland, shielding its owner's face from the assault of Scottish sunshine and failing to shield it from the more determined assault of Scottish rain. It has fished the Wharfe and the Eden and the Ure; it has visited the East Yorkshire chalkstreams, where it was perhaps too humble a hat to feel entirely comfortable along the margins of the Driffield Beck; but no one insulted it and it stayed firmly in place.

It has gone shooting with me for ducks and rabbits and pheasants, though I must confess that I have left it at home on my rare visits to grouse moors, concerned that it might feel its lack of breeding while waiting with me for the birds to come, and while those other hats, all of ancient and impeccable lineage, were stretched out in line over the purple heather on either side of me. It has been spared the spectacle of my attempts to shoot driven grouse, but once or twice it has fallen off my head in amazement when I have swung my gun through the line of some distant speck of a pheasant and brought the bird tumbling to earth. The highest pheasant I ever shot came out of the kale on my syndicate shoot near Settle. I was standing down by the beck when a hen broke back towards the wood, climbing way up into the sky and shining in the

December sun. I do not know what happened, except that the bird fell when I pulled the trigger and that, on this occasion, my hat ended up in the water and was collected by Merlin before he went off to find the pheasant.

More than once, on windy days in spring or autumn, it has floated down the currents of the upper Wharfe. It fell into the river with me not many weeks ago. Last summer it was with me on the Eden when a huge hatch of blue wings brought every trout in the river onto the feed and I caught four two-pounders in little more than an hour. That was undoubtedly its greatest fishing triumph, but it always enjoyed the lesser days, even the fishless ones. It enjoyed going to feed my birds at High Park; it enjoyed the modest sport High Park offers those who shoot there. Certainly High Park is where it felt most at home, but it seems that it will never go there again, unless perhaps it is now there permanently because it stayed behind one afternoon when its owner came back to Sedbergh without making sure that it was sitting on his head.

I cannot remember when it was last on top of me. Missing things often turn out to have been hiding in the back of the Land Rover, but I have rummaged among waders and walking boots, among landing nets and plastic crows and empty wheat sacks. I have found a box of flies that I thought I had dropped somewhere on the Wharfe; I have thrown away some well-rotted sandwiches and I have recovered two pairs of stockings. Of my hat there has been no sign, and I cannot find it up at school; I have not left it in the pub. It is nowhere to be seen in the flat. It has gone missing before, but then it has always turned up after a day or two. Almost a fortnight has now passed since I last saw my hat and I am beginning to fear that we shall never meet again.

I have not quite abandoned hope. Perhaps I shall find it under the trees at High Park; I may stumble upon it somewhere on the banks of the Wharfe or the Eden. As yet I am refusing to despair and I have not gone into mourning. So far I have refused to put on a replacement, but before long I shall have to renew my acquaintance with the shrunk and crumpled flat cap that was my inseparable companion until just over five years ago. I shall, of course, have to find it first.

Recently we caught up with the crows, just a few of then. Two boys and I shot about a dozen one Sunday afternoon and then hung them from branches round the pens, dangling unattractively on long lengths of baling twine. It was not a good afternoon for crow destruction: there was only a light breeze and they were not mobbing the hoppers as they so often do, but floating over them just on or beyond the limit of range. I am not going to tell you how many cartridges it took me to bring down just four or five birds, although I promise that, when the real shooting starts, I shall keep and publish an honest record of shots fired and birds killed.

The average shooter, we are told, should kill a pheasant with every third cartridge. I think that the average shooter, on familiar ground where he knows the habits of the birds, should do a little better than that, unless of course his familiar ground sends famously tall and testing pheasants up into the sky. At High Park, which is not a shoot with a national reputation, and where it is my friends who are waiting expectantly in those places where the challenging birds come, while their host works the gorse and the rough cover with old Merlin or bad Digby, raising his gun only at those birds that insist on flying the wrong way – at High Park I expect half my shots to find their target. On my syndicate shoot I hope for something similar, but I am satisfied with one for three and there are, of course, days when disappointment sets in early and steadily deepens until it has turned into profoundest gloom.

As a guest I am very undependable. I have stood beneath pheasants in Northumberland and North Yorkshire, waving my gun

at them and knowing that it was only chance that brought the occasional bird down to earth. Undoubtedly it is when the average shooter meets pheasants beyond his usual experience that the limits of his competence are often pitilessly exposed. When the average shooter meets driven grouse it is a meeting that often breeds despair. As a rule he copes better with flighting duck, although teal have the ability to persuade him that he is way below average, especially when the wind is up and they come on the very edge of darkness. Then, in fact, this particular average shooter often finds that he has not missed a single bird, but this is because they have all been to quick for him and he has never even mounted his gun.

This same run-of-the-mill shooter was not on the top of his form the other day while trying to deal with high crows. He was sitting beneath an ash tree up in the long grass round the new pen, smoking his pipe and watching the silent drift of the clouds and of the shadows that were moving beneath them over the surrounding fields. He was happy, even though he had finally acknowledged that he would never see his old cotton hat again and had therefore replaced it with the crumpled flat cap. Long-tailed tits were making wheezing noises in the branches above him; now and then they were joined by foraging parties of finches; a pied wagtail sat in the pale sunshine on a nearby fence-post for a minute or two; and throughout the afternoon there were yellow leaves drifting on the air and sometimes settling at his feet.

All round me in the grass there were young pheasants and, when from time to time a crow flapped over and a shot rang out, they neither batted an eyelid nor stirred a feather. There was a particular bird, a cock now almost in full plumage, that sat all after-noon in a little bowl of dust no more than five yards from me, watching my attempts to kill crows with perfect composure and doubtless concluding that he would not have much to fear from at least one shooter when the time came for him to earn his daily ration

of corn by taking to the wing and flying over the sike once or twice a month.

As I sat there, waiting for the crows and exchanging nods with my cock pheasant, my thoughts turned to hoppers and I decided that, in past seasons, I had kept too many of them round the old pen and on Beck Bank, which are both close to the borders of my little shoot. And last year I should certainly have moved most of the feeders away from the new pen after the end of November; for the land up there is exposed to the winter winds and does not hold many birds once the cover has died down. This year I am gradually moving hoppers away from the pens towards the centre of things. In partic- ular I hope to persuade more birds to frequent the Rise; four feeders are already in place and soon there will be more. There are now only two on Beck Bank; those that formerly hung beside them have leapt over the sike to the edges of the gorse, and some of the hoppers from the vicinity of the old pen have moved down and across the water to line the north side of the wood.

The thinking behind this mass movement of hoppers is that it will encourage birds away from the edges of my shoot, away, above all, from Beck Bank, where they generally fly – or more often run – straight over the boundary fence, and where some will lurk even with no hoppers to entice them there. I want pheasants on the Rise, in the Whins and in the Gutter; I want them on both sides of the wood and in the gorse that spreads over North Bank; for these are all places where flushed birds usually fly over the waiting guns and usually offer sporting shots; some of them are also places where, in the past, there has often been a distinct shortage of birds.

These, anyway, were some of the thoughts that occupied me as I sat near the new pen waiting for crows. It was very pleasant to sit in the sunshine on the edge of a new season, wondering how I could make it better than the last one, devising little schemes or grand

strategies and blithely confident that they would all work. The next four months will show me whether my hopes for a new approach to hopper management have been well-founded. Long before that I shall discover whether the dangling corpses that we left behind us as memorials of a lazy afternoon's sport have persuaded the crows of Stainmore to look elsewhere for their corn. If they prove stubbornly attached to my hoppers, there will, at any rate, be time for one more go at them.

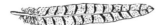

For many years, somewhere near the beginning of a new fishing or shooting season, I have scribbled down a few sentences in my diary expressing my hopes for the months ahead. I like to turn back to them at the season's end and to see how far these hopes and ambitions have been fulfilled. It can, of course, be dispiriting to acknowledge that, once again, I failed to remain calm in the few big drives that pheasant time brought my way; it is distressing to realise that I broke a solemn promise to myself and did not go fishing on at least a hundred days between the beginning of April and the end of September; I always spend less time tying flies than I tell myself that I will; I never remember to keep my temper when bad Digby decides to disgrace himself, so that my wild outbursts only make his behaviour worse.

But there are satisfactions as well as disappointments. I usually find that there have been days at High Park when the bag exceeded my expectations; I discover that there was a promise I did manage to keep by exercising some restraint and only flighting my duck pond once a month; I realise that my May fishing was even better than I had dared to hope; or I remind myself of the January day when I shot all the six birds flushed within range of my gun. But, whether looking back through my fishing or my shooting diary, I am always forced to admit that some of the hopes that accompanied the beginning of a new season were foolish hopes, were no more than fantasies that should have been repressed as soon as they first rose up in my mind.

My first hope for the coming season's shooting is probably of this sort; it almost certainly belongs to the world of make-believe and, almost inevitably, it involves Mr Blair; for I hope that he will wake up one morning in the next few weeks; I hope that, as he sips his morning cup of tea, chatting away to Cherie and the kids about his chances of governing Britain for the next thirty years, he will suddenly grasp the profound beauty that lies at the heart of country sports and, like St Paul on the road to Damascus, turn in a moment from a persecutor into an apostle. Perhaps he will go on to establish the Sedgefield Hunt. He may, with all the generous spirit of the convert, invite Anne Widdecombe to share the mastership with him; she has the right sort of voice for the hunting field and would look splendid on top of a horse capable of carrying her; and perhaps Mr Campbell will abandon spin-doctoring and at last find honest employment as a whipper-in? But, if Mr Blair refuses to take up fox-hunting, my hope is that he will suddenly tire of politics and devote the rest of his life to the service of the Church of England; for, if he does this, then no one will ever again take the slightest notice of anything that he feels obliged to say.

My Blair-centred hopes are certainly an idle fantasy, as too, I suppose, are those for my dogs: my hope that Merlin's arthritis will relent or miraculously disappear, so that he will once again be able to thrust himself through the gorse at High Park with all the manic energy of his prime, showing no signs of stiffness or fatigue at the end of the day, but eager to start all over again or at least to go flighting as the light fails.

I hope that I shall not have to curse Digger a single time in the course of the whole season, never denouncing him as the Hound from Hell or the Prince of Darkness. Throughout August he was with me at High Park and most afternoons I took him in search of rabbits. He behaved almost impeccably, sitting to flush like a field trial champion and gazing at me reproachfully, as though wondering why I found it necessary to blow frantic blasts on my whistle, then to roar 'sit' and 'steady' and 'leave it' in a voice that made thunder sound kind. He looked as though he could not begin to understand why I was making such a commotion, all because a rabbit had leapt up from beneath his nose or merely because a cock pheasant had clattered noisily onto the wing. He looked as though he was surprised and disappointed that I could doubt his steadiness in the face of temptations that he had learned to resist whole seasons ago. He even remained sitting, and gazing at his master complacently, when the sight of a running rabbit was accompanied by the sound of a gun.

I am unconvinced by Digger's apparent reform. I suspect that he will behave differently when the gun is aimed at the rabbit and when the rabbit rolls over in the grass. I know that I rushed him into the shooting field and that it is usually the excitement inspired by loud bangs and by falling birds that makes me wish I had called him Mandelson. I think Digger is too old a dog to turn over new leaves, but I cannot help hoping and it is just possible that he will surprise me.

There is a less remote hope concerning a little extension of the kingdom; at present it is almost a secret hope and I shall not mention it again unless it turns into a hope fulfilled. But my hopes for the weather do not need to be hidden away. For my first shoot right at the end of October I want a day of serene autumn sunshine; it will not be the best weather for showing early-season birds, but then my first shoot is little more than a rehearsal; it is the day when my pheasants learn that High Park is a more dangerous place than it has seemed to them for the last twelve weeks; I like the sun to shine on their feathers as they fly over the sike; I like the leaves to glow above us as we sit by the meadow gate and eat our sandwiches and sip our drams. The day for wind will be my second day in the middle of November; ideally it will be a stiff breeze from the South, for then it will lift birds and speed them over the guns, most of whom will be the boys who help me with the work at High Park during term-time.

My third shoot is as near as I get to a big shoot; it is High Park's version of a grande battue, representing my attempt to thank one or two friends who regularly invite me to shoot their more extensive and more abundantly stocked coverts. My third shoot might see as many as twenty pheasants in the bag at the end of the day, twenty pheasants and a few rabbits and perhaps a woodcock or two. On my third shoot I should once again like to see broken clouds moving purposefully through the sky and to watch my birds crossing the sike with the wind in their tails. And then they will be allowed to rest until my fiftieth birthday, when I am hoping that they will rise in ones and twos and threes and then hurtle over the waiting guns to salute my half century. The day should be one of bitter cold and biting frost, with a sharp wind and a grey sky and rime still thick on the gorse at noon; it should be a day suggestive of the old age that is creeping up on me, a day for mittened fingers and stamping feet and defiant enjoyment on the edge of decrepitude.

Thereafter I would have frost in the earth until the end of January, for after those first four shoots it is time to forget about organised days and to harass my birds – with or without a friend or two – whenever the spirit moves me; and the spirit might move me as often as once a week and, having moved me, it might very well send me home with an empty game bag, for it is impossible to hold birds into the New Year on my little patch of land unless hard

weather lends me a helping hand. Frost is good in January, but snow, the sort of snow that lies and freezes and seems to become almost a part of the earth it covers, snow would be best of all.

Such, at any rate, are my hopes for the weather. My next hope concerns me and my conduct both as host and shooter, for I hope that I shall always put my guests in the best spots at each of my little drives, and I hope that I shall never again yield to temptation by shooting an unsporting bird merely to help the progress of the season's total at High Park. I do not lift my gun to unworthy birds on other men's shoots; it is demeaning and shameful to do it on my own. It is a fault of which I have sometimes been guilty in the past and I am determined that it will never happen again.

I also hope that I shall soon find some cartridges loaded with bismuth shot and then take them in search of the season's first mallard. And I hope that, when I am the guest of friends, I shall shoot well enough not to feel ashamed of my presence in the line. I hope that, at the end of shooting days, especially those at High Park, all who have been part of them will go home enriched by their sport and grateful for the enrichment.

And finally I return to Mr Blair, for I fear that my earlier hopes for him are hopes without foundation; and so my final hope is that, if he insists on continuing his persecution of those who find a great beauty, and some part of the meaning of their lives, in the historic ritual of the hunt – I hope, if he is finally willing to set a higher value upon political expediency than upon individual freedom, that the spirits of mighty hunters from the past, the spirits of Trollope and Surtees and Sassoon, perhaps even of old John Peel himself together with Squire Osbaldeston flushed from his port, will rise before him as he sleeps and fill his dreams with eloquent and angry complaints.

I hope that the sad baying of a thousand hounds, all condemned to die as soon as the sport to which they belong has been declared a crime, will wake him in the darkness and fill his heart with shame. And perhaps Reynard himself will trot into one of his dreams and ask him what he thinks he is up to, and why he is so determined to turn the legendary Mr Tod, a character with a place in the hearts of all those who have pursued him down the years, into just another animal, just another pest to be destroyed with cold efficiency: a creature become suddenly as ignoble as a stoat in the bottom of a dry-stone wall or a rat in the stinking darkness of a drain.

Just before the end of the month I finally ran two boxes of bismuth cartridges to earth in Penrith. It cost me twenty five pounds to get my hands on them, but I should have been willing to part with twice as much; for they meant that at last I could pay my first predatory visit of the season to the little flight pond that lies in the hollow of a field just over my boundary at High Park. I drove back to Sedbergh singing at the wheel of the Land Rover, singing and dreaming of mallard-shapes circling overhead in the deepening light, circling above me and then dropping down towards the water where I love to wait for them as the light fades. This singing and dreaming was on a Saturday afternoon; in the course of it I decided that, if things went to plan, the coming Tuesday would be the evening of my first flight.

Tuesday did not bring ideal conditions for flighting duck; it brought weather of a sort I much prefer, especially early in the season when duck are less wary and the wind is less important. Tuesday brought a very quiet evening, with grey light gathered beneath a ridged and furrowed cover of cloud. It was a soft, still evening with damp air, and the colours were gentle impressions of

green and brown and yellow and grey; there were no sharp outlines. It was the sort of evening when the darkness comes as an almost imperceptible blurring and thickening of the light, seeping out of the moist earth and spreading itself very slowly round me, as I sit on an up-ended plastic bucket beneath a gnarled crab-apple tree, sitting and smoking and waiting patiently for the first sound of wings.

Almost always I arrive far too early at my flight pond; it is a planned rather than an impatient sort of earliness, because the waiting is half the pleasure of it all: sitting there on my black bucket as the light fails, as pheasants disturb the mood of the evening and clatter noisily up to roost, as crows flock past on lazy wings towards their dormitories in the trees. On warm September evenings there are still midges dancing in the last light. Sometimes a young buzzard comes flapping into the pines behind me – temptation, if it comes to me, is virtuously resisted – and always there is a robin whistling very quietly somewhere along the line of the hedge. Now and then a pigeon passes overhead, and very slowly the sounds turn almost to silence, with only a faint stirring of the leaves above me and the ceaseless murmur of the sike behind. Somewhere a cow bellows; a roe deer barks in the wood, and all the time shapes grow dimmer and sink slowly into the rising darkness while, sitting there on my bucket beneath the leaves, sitting there with fallen crab-apples all round my feet, I am absorbed into the hushed peace of the night.

It is this peace that draws me to flight ponds: the peace and the strangely complementary expectancy that fills it as I sit there waiting for the sound of wings. And the mood tightens to excite-ment as soon as that pulsing rhythm is heard beating invisibly in the darkening sky; and when sound turns into seeing, when those long-necked silhouettes are suddenly before me on their cupped wings, dropping purposefully towards the water, then for a second the

56

excitement explodes and one or two shots ring out. There is to flighting a wider range of feeling than comes to any other form of shooting; to experience the full richness of it you must be there early. I was late on Tuesday and it was still wonderful.

The evening was already far gone when I came to Low Park Pond. I had been delayed at school and already there were duck, perhaps a dozen of them, feeding along the edges of the water. They flew off quacking and I settled down hurriedly on my bucket, settling Merlin beside me and comforting myself with the thought that he should still be able to come flighting with me when grown too old and too stiff for steep banks and thick stands of gorse. Pheasants were at roost and there was no sound from them. The air rustled faintly as the last black shapes of crows moved overhead. Duck should come only when the crows have found shelter in the trees; they should come only when the shooter begins to wonder whether they will come at all. Wild weather brings them sooner; they are often earlier at the beginning of the season and, if disturbed while feeding, they will often attempt a prompt return.

On Tuesday there was no time for quiet thoughts and tobacco among the fallen fruit. Suddenly, somewhere above the lazy flapping of the crows, I heard a more urgent and wheeling rhythm of wings, and mixed in with it was the nervous mutter of duck talk. They were certainly wary birds; they were surely the same birds that I had put off the pond only a few minutes ago; but the wide high circles became lower and narrower, while the sound of wings grew nearer and louder, until suddenly two shapes were planing down through the greyness, shapes with wide wings and broad bills and long necks; and then there were two shots and both shapes fell; and then Merlin bounded off to bring them both back to me.

I was in love with bismuth, for my first two shots with it had given me a right and left; very soon a dim shape crossed the far side of the pond; a third shot rang out; the shape folded and fell and Merlin had soon found it for me. By now I felt that I should never miss a duck again, until this delusion was blown away by a foolish shot at a high shape right above me, a shape that, if I had waited, would soon have turned into a much nearer though still sporting shape; it was a wild swipe through the sky, with overhanging branches preventing a proper swing or a second barrel. It was a foolish shot and it persuaded me that three duck were enough for one evening; for, if I crept away while the mallard were still coming in, I should be able to think of another flight in as little as three weeks; and then, I promised myself, I should not arrive on the edge of darkness but at the first deepening of the light, ready to sit on my bucket and smoke my pipe while the shadows rose, while the pheasants shouted and the crows flapped to roost, ready to drink in the peace that is the prelude of the excitement to come.

So ended the season's first flight. The mallard have been plucked and stored in the freezer; they are plump birds and they will be honoured, at their eating, with a bottle of Clos l'Arlot '91. I shall drink a toast in their honour – you will have realised by now that I am addicted to little rituals of this sort – thanking them for the sweetness of their flesh, for the wonderful sound of their wings and for the sudden shape of them against a grey and darkening sky. I may announce to my guests that the way they reached my table was full of beauty, inspiring in the man who shot them a deep sense of gratitude for his presence and his place in the created world, and a deep thankfulness that he could find flesh for his belly in a manner that filled him with both peace and praise.

The season's first flight left me with happy thoughts for the next two or three days and my mind was so full of the shapes of mallard that it had no room left for images of Mr Tony Blair. But then, one morning long before daylight, I woke up sweating and switched on the light and realised with indescribable relief that it

had only been a dream. I was not really confined in a room with the Prime Minister and no one else for company; I could breathe easy and calm myself and go back to sleep again. There was no need to panic or to scream; there was no necessity to look under the bed in order to make quite certain that he was not there. It had been nothing but a morbid secretion of the subconscious mind.

I did go back to sleep again and, the next day being Thursday, in the afternoon I went out to High Park to feed my birds. It was very pleasant in the sunshine and I enjoyed telling myself that my pheasants were unusually well on for late September birds. I carried sacks of wheat to the hoppers, filled them and then sat down to rest and smoke for a time. I watched the leaves falling and floating down the sike. I gathered mushrooms from my top pastures and a few late blackberries from the brambles round the old pen. In the middle of all this my thoughts strayed back to the hideous dream of the past night and I began to wonder how I should react if I really were locked in a room with Tony Blair as my sole companion.

I know that I should immediately be seized by a frantic urge to escape: to some place, to any place in the world where I could once again breathe a Blairless atmosphere. I should rattle doors in the desperate hope that someone had forgotten to turn the key. The thought of Wormwood Scrubs, or even of the Millennium Dome, would be a vision of paradise and, inspired by this vision, I should clamber up to window sills to see if there were bars beyond the glass. Boards would be wrenched from the floor in the hope of secret tunnels leading to uncontaminated air. And finally, if all attempts at departure failed, I should cower trembling in a corner of our room and beg Mr Blair, whatever he might do, not to smile.

After a time I suppose I should get a grip on myself. I should try to engage Mr Blair in conversation. We might talk about claret for a while. We could, of course, talk about the weather or the Euro.

Mr Blair would doubtless entertain me with his vision of a new, modern Britain under his new and modern leadership. I should then ask him why hunting with hounds had no place in his brand new vision; I should also explain to him that shooting men were uncertain of their future in a Britain governed by New Labour, feeling threatened and unloved and fearful that their traditional freedoms were likely to be circumscribed by hostile legislation. I should have a word or two to say to Mr Blair about the inanity of his new regulations restricting the use of lead shot; I should point out to him that there is no need for the flighters of small ponds to spend a fortune on new and modern cartridges, since, back in the bad old days, all the shot from our unreformed cartridges fell way out in the fields, nowhere near any water, and was never ingested by a single duck.

I should be mistrustful of any assurances that came from the lips of Mr Blair and, when the moment seemed right, I should seize my opportunity and try to persuade him that not all hunters and shooters were primitive landowners or half-witted peasants who knew no better way of passing time than to pass it by killing things. I should try to make Mr Blair understand what it is that makes and keeps us sportsmen. If he could appreciate our motives he might be less inclined to disapprove. I am not sure that all hunters and shooters and fishers could clearly articulate what it is that holds them in such happy bondage; I am not sure that I can do it myself but, in conversation with Mr Blair, I should make a start with two words, which would be beauty and love. This would probably surprise Mr Blair, but just for the moment I have forgotten about him.

To consider beauty first, it is, of course, true that our sports belong to beautiful places: to moors and lakes and rivers and wooded valleys. Some of the happiest moments in my life have been spent sitting by a flight pond or standing at a peg by the side of a covert or lying by a river with my rod in the grass beside me, always

at times of resting from active sport or waiting for it to begin, but at times when the beauty around me, penetrating my senses with a sudden and unusual sharpness, has called forth a response of marvel and thankfulness. This is not the sort of beauty with which I am now concerned; I am thinking instead of the beauty of the sports themselves and the way this beauty enriches all those who help to make it.

One of the reasons why fishing does not meet with general disapproval is that even those who know almost nothing about it dimly sense that it is a beautiful activity. They may have seen anglers casting flies on the television; they may have stood on bridges and watched fly-fishers busy in the pools below them; they will have responded to the graceful movements of rod and line and to the quiet sounds they make as they curve and curl through the air. A fisherman complements the beauty of still or running water because, in his own way, he makes beauty himself. His aim, of course, is to catch and often to kill the living beauty of his rivers and lakes; but because there are no loud bangs and no hounds giving wild tongue, and because fishers are usually solitary and blend so peacefully into their surroundings, people can believe that they go fishing to feed the spirit as well as to fill their creels; and so they are happy to smile on them and allow them a few trout or an odd salmon as their reward for a long day under the sky; which is, I suppose, why a member of parliament could introduce a bill to outlaw hunting with hounds, while at the same time insisting to us that he was a normal person by pointing out that he loved to catch fish.

The quiet beauties of fishing are to an extent appreciated by those who do not fish themselves. It is recognised that these beauties lie at the heart of the fisher's attachment to his sport; but many of the people who are happy to grant this would be surprised, and quite possibly angry, to be told that our sport as shooters also concerns itself with the search for beauty and for peace and with the creation of them both. There is, for example, great beauty in the sight of a spaniel hunting a hedge or quartering a rough bank. There is sudden and gorgeous beauty in the rising of a cock pheasant from cover; and a high driven bird, with the wind in his tail and the sun in his feathers, curls and shines in the sky with a wild and a challenging beauty. And what of the tilting, dipping and lifting beauty of the dark shapes of grouse as they skim the heather on their way to the butts? And the shooter himself makes beauty with his gun, for that sudden transition from flight to fall is strangely beautiful; and often his dog makes beauty of another sort with the grace of an efficient retrieve.

It is such things that make us shooters, not the lust for blood or a perverted pleasure in the spectacle of death. As for the killing we feel that if, as is still generally agreed, it is right for men to eat the flesh of animals, then it is surely right and proper for men to do the killing themselves rather than to expect others to do it for them, to do it moreover in a way that is sudden and seemly, to do it with respect and with wonder and with reverence.

And this brings me at last to love, which, you will remember, was the second of the two words that I thought would help Mr Blair, and others with no understanding of fieldsports, to approach the sportsman's experience. For the sportsman most certainly loves his quarry; the fisher loves the spotted trout the river gives to him, or the great silver salmon with lice still clinging – proof that it is fresh from the sea. The shooter loves the mallard and the teal that fill the darkening sky with the excitement of beating wings; he loves his pheasants in the brief splendour of their flight; he loves the myste-rious woodcock and the humble running rabbit. This sportsman's love does not bring the twined and knotted and often painful attach-ments that bind him to some members of his own kind; nor does it inspire the sentimental affection he feels for tame animals,

especially for his dogs; he loves his quarry for its beauty, for its cunning, for the speed of its flight, for the sweetness of its flesh, for all the joy it brings him in the pursuit of his sport; he reveres it as a part of the created world to which he himself belongs and upon which his existence depends. His sport and his quarry are, in fact, a sort of symbol to him of his place in the order of things: of man driven by need and desire to exploit and to kill other animals, driven at the same time by a different and uniquely human compulsion to respect his fellow creatures and to transform desire and necessity into something beautiful. Through his sport he learns part of what it is to be a man; he learns a truth about our involvement with animals that is often forgotten: that we have always killed them to protect or to sustain our own lives, that we have long and rightly thought of them as essentially different from ourselves, but that, even in the killing, we must look on them as part of the glory of creation and so worthy of high regard and, yes, even of love; of that strong and natural emotion that grows from a bond of need. It is, of course, a sort of general love: it is love of the species rather than love of the individual.

Fieldsports preserve something of the essence of this ancient relationship between man and animals, together with some of the ancient reverence that belongs to it. This is why I believe so firmly in their rightness and think that, far from being anomalous barbarities, they restore to those who take part in them a true understanding of man's place in nature. Returning to Mr Blair and our imaginary confinement I do not imagine for a moment that I should convert him to my way of thinking; if I could convert the nation he would follow soon enough, for that is generally Mr Blair's way. But, were I locked up in a room with Mr Blair and escape proved impossible, I should spend the hours of my agony trying to persuade him that men who shoot and hunt are not all callous murderers, that they are men in search of beauty, that their hearts are often stirred with gratitude and love.

I suppose Mr Blair might say that he understood my thoughts on shooting without agreeing with them, but did not see how they applied to hunting since, given the fact that foxes are famously inedible, their slaughter cannot be justified by appeal to the stomach and its needs. I should be ready for Mr Blair; in response to his objection I should first praise all the beauties of the chase: the pageantry of the meet, the sound and sight of hounds, the power and the grace of the horses, the thrilling music of the horn. After explaining that hunting is a subtle and complicated art, admitting at the same time that my understanding of it is very shallow, I should point out that, although foxes are not slain to provide the Sunday roast at No.10 Downing Street, they belong to that class of animals upon which man has always waged war, namely those that threaten his livestock: his lambs and his poultry and his game. I should argue that fox-hunting has transubstantiated the necessity to control predators into a ritual that stirs the heart of the hunter, not with the urge for slaughter or with longing for the sight of blood, but with admiration for the speed and the cunning of his quarry and with delight in the exhilarating beauties of his sport. Reverence and love are perhaps the wrong words with which to describe the hunter's relationship with the fox. The appropriate analogy here is the respect a soldier feels for a skilled and fearless adversary; admiration and respect are the correct words. Why, I should ask Mr Blair, was he so eager to abolish something that, far from revealing man in his depravity, reveals the power of his imagination and his ability to transform dull necessity into ritual and beauty and art.

It would then be time to change direction, time to ask Mr Blair how on earth he thought foxes would benefit from the abolition of hunting. Did he think that fewer of them would be killed? 'Cui bono?' I would cry. Was he eager to improve the lot of foxes in his modern Britain or was he anxious to protect the feelings – and keep the votes – of those sensitive souls to whom the very thought of the hunt and the kill was so profoundly upsetting? Did he know

anything about the sport that he was now proposing to abolish? Was he willing to learn anything about it before he declared it a crime? Did he have a pleasant time in Tuscany? How many mass murderers was he proposing to release next week? Why would he not let me eat oxtail stew any longer?

I do hope that Cherie, or one of those nice spin-doctors, would take pity on us before too long and unlock the door. Mr Blair would doubtless be just as relieved as his fellow prisoner. He would hurry off to continue modernising Britain. I would rush to High Park, where I would sit above the old pen and smoke heavily until I began to feel normal again, breathing in the sharp evening air between deep inhalations of smoke and looking forward to my first pheasant shoot in just over three weeks time.

CHAPTER FOUR

OCTOBER

*Pheasant gazing; the business of
keepering; more solitary duck flighting;
final check before the first pheasant shoot;
70 extra acres; the first day*

Watching pheasants is one of my favourite autumn activities; usually they are my own pheasants, but, if my way takes me past roadside coverts, I am always ready to stop the Land Rover and to spend five minutes watching somebody else's birds, comparing them with my own and concluding that their tails are far shorter and that it will take them a whole fortnight longer to be ready for the gun. I enjoy watching anybody's pheasants, but it is my own that give me the greatest pleasure, especially in early October sunshine, when they are still almost a month away from the first shoot but are already almost mature, with the hens now difficult to distinguish from last year's birds, while the cocks parade this way and that, perfecting their strut in plumage that is still waiting for its final burnish, for those last strokes of polished splendour that always seem to me a part of the same process that, as October progresses, turns leaves to yellow and russet and to gold.

Watching pheasants is good at any time of the year; it is, of course, an important part of the keeper's job. It is by sitting and watching his birds that he checks on their health, but he cannot help finding pleasure in this restful part of the day's routine. On hot afternoons it is a delight to watch poults rubbing themselves in the dust. It is amusing to observe the first signs of male aggression as young cocks face up to each other, fluffing out their feathers and flicking their heads from side to side; and there is always something comical about the way a pheasant walks, with that slow raising of the feet and that search for a dignity that is never quite achieved: that striving after a solemn progress which always remains faintly ridiculous.

I enjoy watching my pheasants at any time of the year; but autumn is much the best time, because in autumn you can look at them as they are and think of them as they were only a few weeks ago: you can compare birds, now looking almost as pheasants should look, with the awkward youngsters that so recently inhabited your pens. You can do this and at the same time you can tell yourself that the time of preparation is now almost past, that the time for sport has almost come. And so it was that, a few days ago, I hobbled up to the old pen, not to feed or water my birds, but just to sit down and take a look at those of them that were still in or round their old home and still willing to submit themselves to inspection.

I am afraid the labours of release have been too much for me, which was the reason for the hobble. I blame those five-gallon drums full of water, half-heaved, half-dragged up the steep slope from the sike by a man only two or three months away from his fiftieth birthday; I blame them in particular for the slips and slides they provoked on wet days when the slope was particularly treacherous. I have twisted something in my back, twisted or trapped or strained it, and, by way of revenge, it sends shooting pains running down my right leg. At present I am a pitiful sight, limping into my classroom or dragging myself to the pub or hobbling up to the pens to watch my pheasants for half an hour. Perhaps, in preparation for next season's release, I should go into training a month before my birds are due to arrive.

I shall begin by asking discreetly for directions to the school gymnasium. After finding where it is I shall make furtive visits at times when no one else is likely to be there; I shall spend vigorous hours lifting heavy objects and groaning with the effort of it all. In my ambition to provide myself with a body equal to the demands of a month's daily pheasant care, I shall climb onto exercise bikes and take my seat on rowing machines. Away from the gymnasium, sit-ups and press-ups will become a regular feature of the day's routine. I have never been much interested in muscles, but I realise now that it will have to change; thank God it will not have to change before next July.

Anyway, it was worth the winces and the feelings of premature decrepitude that came to me as I struggled up the fifty or so yards of Pheasant Hill. Once settled on the summit, looking down on the pen with my gammy leg stretched out more or less comfortably in front of me, I found that there were many pheasants lurking in the grass or feeding at the hoppers or sitting dusting in the sun. My heart went out to a lame cock limping round the pen; he was almost the only pheasant left on the inside of the wire. I thought that I recognised him as a bird that had been injured in his crate on the journey to High Park, a bird that could scarcely walk when he first arrived on my land. I never expected him to survive more than a few days, which was why, for kindness' sake, I was tempted to knock him on the head; but something stayed my hand and the weeks passed and still he was there, undaunted by his infirmity and getting bigger in spite of it. Now he was as big as any of the pheasants I could see, with a tail that would have done credit to a November cock; and the sight of him, limping on his way like a Long John Silver of a

pheasant, the sight of him was a deep pleasure to me and inspired some superficial sense of fellow-feeling.

As I sat there, anyway, testing my right leg for twinges and blowing smoke at the flies, I decided that it was time to declare this year's release an unqualified success. There had been almost no disease and it had been dealt with very easily; known losses amounted to no more than three or four birds, and the survivors – approximately 146 of them – had grown more quickly than I could remember. Things had never gone more smoothly at High Park and the first shoot was now only weeks away. That same evening I should have to ring friends and fix a date somewhere in the last week of October; but, as I sat there above the pen and watched my pheasants occupying themselves so peacefully in the sunshine, I did not want to think of the sound of guns or the sight of falling birds. They would be heard and seen soon enough, and I was happy that it would not happen for a few more weeks; for the truth is that, sitting there watching and smoking, I was feeling protective rather than predatory.

It was probably the sight of that limping cock and it is not a feeling that will last. One afternoon before long I shall spot one of his long-tailed friends beneath the leaves, or catch sight of a hen slinking into the gorse; then all at once I shall realise that the time for watching is past. I know a few amateur keepers who never really relish shooting their own birds. I confess that I am not one of them. The transformation from protector to predator seems, in my case, to happen quite naturally as part of the cycle of the year. But I turn into a duck-hunter before I begin to think of pheasants in the same way; there will be another flight at Low Park Pond before the first of my pheasants falls out of the sky.

Tuesday is my preferred evening for duck ponds. This is partly because professional duties often invade other evenings of the week and insist that I should renounce the sacred pleasures of flighting. But the reason I so relish sitting by the edge of a flight pond on Tuesday evenings is mainly a social one; and this is because each Tuesday evening during term ends for me among a gathering of friends, assembled – not before half past nine – to drink wine together, to enjoy each other's company and to sit round a table and eat food. When it is my turn to produce the wine and the food I leave my ponds to the darkness and the duck; but when someone else is busy crushing cloves of garlic and opening bottles of claret, on those Tuesday evenings I often leave Sedbergh as the sun dips, hoping to return an hour or two later with enough mallard in my bag to feed the members of the Tuesday Club when I am next their host.

My love affair with bismuth continues. Last Tuesday evening I flighted Low Park Pond again and eight cartridges brought me a record bag of six mallard. The pond is only about a hundred yards from the road and, even as I was collecting the dog from the back of the Land Rover, I saw a pair of duck dropping down to the water. I crept up towards the pond, sitting Merlin fifty yards or so away from it. At least a dozen birds rose at the sight of me and, though my first shot was high of its target, the second found its mark and Merlin had soon brought a drake to hand.

Thereafter there was plenty of time to sit under the old crab and watch the day fade all round me. Flighting conditions were even less promising than on my first visit, for there was no wind at all and the sky was bright; but it was beautiful and it was a blessing just to be sitting there, with mittens on my fingers for protection from the sharp air, with steam on Merlin's breath and with a new hat of sorts on my head, a gift from the same journalist who gave me the peerless hat that has been missing now for something like six weeks. Its substitute is also of green cotton and of foreign origin, but it is

much floppier and it has a ridiculously wide brim which might, I suppose, be useful in the hotter parts of Australia, or even by an English troutstream on a burning summer's day; but it is certainly out of place on the edge of a Cumbrian flight pond on a chilly evening in October. I do not think I shall ever learn to love my new hat, even though its first evening on my head was an evening of such memorable sport.

There was plenty of time for me to savour the remains of the day, to watch tumbling flocks of jackdaws and to listen to their peals of evening laughter as they flocked to roost at the end of another day spent plundering my hoppers. Then a heron flapped past on creaking wings; and all the time I could hear my pheasants shouting good night to each other, while gradually the air grew colder and forms very slowly lost their sharpness. The gammy leg was aching a bit but not enough to discompose me. Meanwhile the tall ash tree across the field became more and more blurred, while gradually the willows turned into dark impressions of branches. The rabbits that had fled my arrival came back out into the field, like hopping shadows, to start feeding again. Low wisps of cloud lost their last fire. Only the thin moon was sharper and brighter than it had been half an hour ago, and the beck seemed to be gurgling a little more loudly now that it was almost invisible.

It was very peaceful sitting on my bucket and waiting for the duck. I crushed a few rotten apples with my boots. I thought of my first pheasant day in less than a week and wondered how the birds would fly. I looked forward to supper at the end of flight and, being a bit of a wine-snob, hoped that my host would be in one of his generous moods. I even said a few prayers (a flight pond, incidentally, although it must be a flight pond before the beginning of flight, a flight pond in the failing light of a calm autumn evening is the ideal setting for the outmoded habit of prayer).

I may have been muttering a Hail Mary or an Our Father when the first duck dropped onto the pond; it put an immediate end to my devotions and, for about twenty minutes, the air was full of the sound and the shapes and the excitement of the flight. The mallard came in ones and twos and in parties of half a dozen and more. Some flew straight in; others circled nervously. Most of them appeared from behind, but a few came low from the right or the left and were suddenly in front of me on wide wings.

It would be wrong of me to pretend that they were difficult shots. A flighter takes the chances that come to him and these were mostly duck that should not have been missed, although there was a pleasing right and left and a long going-away bird. But there were no shapes plummeting from way up in the sky and, when I missed a much lower shape, partly because it was now almost too dark to see, I decided that six mallard were quite enough for one evening and left as quickly as possible, telling myself that Low Park Pond would not hear another shot, except for distant ones aimed at my pheasants, for at least a month.

The pleasures of flighting are great and they are best enjoyed with only a dog for company. I am a convivial man but I prefer flight ponds unpeopled by anyone except me. It is only in this loneliness that I absorb the damp peace that comes like an invisible mist from still water as it turns grey and then darkens under the approach of night. And the duck, when they come, come like secrets of the night, and such secrets are best appreciated alone. I think this is why, whenever possible, I choose Tuesdays for my flighting; it means that, on the same evening, I can indulge both the solitary and the sociable sides of my nature. I enjoy being alone, I enjoy the sense of complete apartness that comes over me as the night falls very slowly and the duck begin to flight; but I enjoy it much more when I know that in an hour or two it will turn into claret and conversation.

I think I am at one in this with many sportsmen; for, although I never met any of the legendary East Anglian fowlers of the generation before my own, from what I have read of their exploits I get the impression that these great duck hunters of the past thought that the perfect plan for an evening's pleasure was to commune with nature on the marsh, shooting a dozen or two fowl as part of the process, then to seek out a smoke-filled tap room and busy themselves with ten or twelve pints of Charles West's best bitter beer. My procedure is more restrained and a trifle more refined; essentially it is of the same sort.

There are, of course, other advantages to solitary flighting that are very plain and very practical. On a small pond a single shooter is much less likely to frighten incoming duck than are two or three or four. A single shooter, moreover, given that there is only one of him, is much less likely to forget himself, surrendering to excitement or frustration by firing at birds that are still circling and still undecided whether or not to come in. Another recommendation is that your single shooter has a free field of fire; he is not worried about shooting his friend's birds or, much more importantly, about shooting his friend. He can take his duck with a delightful lack of constraint.

Best of all is that the solitary flighter can send his dog to gather each bird as it falls, which he must never do when it might ruin the sport of others. When I am alone Merlin always retrieves during flight; he may, as he dashes this way and that in search of his prey, frighten incoming birds; and it is sometimes necessary, if a particular bird proves elusive, to call him in and try again when flight is over. But undoubtedly he picks wounded duck that would be lost if they were left for half an hour or even for ten minutes. As long, moreover, as Merlin has retrieved successfully and there are no more duck to be gathered, there is no need for that concluding search with torch and whistle: a search that confirms every late-

coming duck in his suspicion that Low Park Pond is a place to avoid for the rest of the season. If a flighter's duck are already in his bag when he has finished shooting, then he can go quickly and quietly, so that birds coming later than the darkness will think his pond the perfect place to fill their bellies; and before long their friends will be joining them, and once again the edge of darkness will be full of the sound of wings.

I was late for the Tuesday Club the other night. When I got back to Sedbergh there were the duck to hang in the shed. Old Merlin needed drying off and I thought that I should be more presentable if I had splashed round in the bath for ten minutes. Ten minutes turned into quarter of an hour. Then I wrote up my shooting diary before my memories of the flight lost their sharpness and, of course, I leafed back through the pages to remind myself of flights from earlier seasons. There was some more random leafing as well but, in spite of it all, I was still only half an hour late. By ten o'clock I was gurgling red wine and chatting away; and, as I gurgled and chatted and stuffed food into my mouth – I was very hungry and there may have been some lack of delicacy to my performance with the knife and fork – anyway, as I feasted on great lumps of roast lamb and washed them down with noisy gulps of wine, I was filled with a sense of private celebration as my mind kept turning back to the loneliness of Low Park Pond, to the duck that had come to it as the night fell and to the half dozen of them that had fallen from the sky and come home with me.

One of the few rules of the Tuesday Club is that it breaks up no later than midnight. The church clock was striking twelve as I walked home, feeling deeply content and reflecting that the two halves of my evening had perfectly and most delightfully comple-mented each other. I had shot six mallard. I had filled my belly with food. I had talked with my friends and enjoyed their company and drunk the best part of a bottle of wine. It had not been claret or

burgundy but there had been nothing wrong with it; it had soothed the ache of my gammy leg and it had helped to call forth those images of still water and of flighting and falling duck. It had all been enough for one night and I decided not to have a whisky before going to bed.

Two days before my first shoot, which is always in our half-term at the end of October, I went out to High Park to fill hoppers and to wander among my birds, checking that everything was ready and making sure that nothing had gone disastrously wrong. I went for these practical reasons, but I also went because it has turned into a private ritual for me: this walking of my boundaries just before the shooting begins; it is my acknowledgement that release-time is over, that growing time is past and that the time for the harvest has finally come. I go up to the pens and remember those mornings when they were full of gawky poults; I look at cock pheasants, now with glowing plumage and with long tails; I look at graceful hens retreating shyly into cover and I give thanks for their survival and their growth, for the beauty of their autumn presence on my land and for the quiet sense of fulfilment that this brings to me. It is Catlow's harvest festival although, unlike other such celebrations, it happens before the harvest begins. It is one of the happiest days of Catlow's year.

This time it was even happier than usual. I shall reveal the reason shortly but, even without this special cause for rejoicing, the day was so beautiful that it would have been impossible not to praise; it was sunny and calm, with a few very brief showers that shone as they fell and made the earth itself shine more brightly with their falling. In the sky and over the land there was that sense of fragile serenity that belongs to still and shining days in late October.

The leaves have been slow to colour this autumn but, for my harvest festival at High Park, they were at last flushing red and russet and copper and yellow. And there were deep drifts of curled green leaves under every ash, with black drifts under all the birches; but although there were many stripped branches pointing to the sky, although there was light under the trees where in August there had been shadows and rare beams of dusty sunshine, it was still only the aspens that were bare, while under the larches my hands and my face were brushed by the soft falling of orange needles in countless profusion.

Everywhere I went, after almost three weeks without rain, there was a dry rustle under my boots; and everywhere – among the fallen leaves and the fading grass and the brown rushes, on the edges of the gorse, in the tangle of brambles on Beck Bank, all along my sunny southern boundary – everywhere there were pheasants, and pheasants with such tails as I have rarely seen so early in the season. Some of them were skulking under piles of brash; some were strutting under the trees, so that it seemed as though their feathers took some of their colour from the leaves above them; others were walking in the sunshine and scuttled into cover as soon as they saw me; a few even took to the wing.

If I had not known better I should have thought that there were five hundred pheasants settled on my land. I revelled in the sight of each one of them and gave thanks for the kind weather that has helped them to grow so rapidly this year. I saw no foxes but I thanked them in their absence for finding their food away from my pens; there were three buzzards in the sky and I waved my thanks to them for deciding that pheasants were not to their taste; I also shouted my thanks to the bounding rabbits for breeding as rabbits are meant to breed and so helping the buzzards to turn their thoughts from feathered prey.

I did not thank the hanging remains of the mink that wandered into my traps during release time. I cannot bring myself to think kind thoughts about mink, even about dead ones, although I might, I suppose, have granted them a posthumous pardon for finding the smell of rotting tunny flesh so irresistible. Nor did my grateful thoughts extend to the crows and the jackdaws that, in spite of my feeble efforts to deter them, are still stubbornly insisting on helping themselves to my grain.

But the jackdaws and the crows could not dispel the sunny mood inspired by a bright sky and by the still air, by the coloured leaves and by the sight of so many pheasants. Late in the afternoon I wandered up to the highest of my fields, to the long ten-acre which I call the Hag. Here too there were pheasants in the rushes, and from here I could see virtually the whole of my little kingdom. The sloping fields looked very beautiful under the October sky and it was good to be standing there in the sunshine, with everything spread before me in the wonderful clarity of the slanting autumn light. It was good to see the purple sloes on the blackthorns and to watch the first fieldfares, with their sloe-coloured heads and rumps, settling noisily among them; it was good to see the red haws hanging in thick clusters and to watch a mistle thrush ripping off the berries with a red-stained beak.

It was good to see chaffinches pecking beneath the hoppers round the new pen, while the rabbits bursting from the rushes made me half regret that I had come to my harvest festival without a gun. It was a delight to admire the orange glow of the sun in the larches above the meadow gate; and down by the sike the green tops of the firs were still catching the light, and the sheep in the meadow were throwing shadows ahead of themselves and were very peaceful shapes. The sudden cackle of a pheasant turned my thoughts back to sport; I told myself that, as a shooter and releaser of pheasants, I had now managed one half of my role: the release was truly over and it

had gone wonderfully well. In looking back over those weeks, during which my birds had turned from ungainly poults into mature and elegant pheasants, I was filled with a sense of quiet satisfaction and of thankfulness.

In looking forward to the pleasures and excitements of sport with those same birds – pleasures that best belong to frosty mornings with frozen gateways and to flaming afternoon skies, to heaving woods where pheasants rise with a clatter and then hurtle down the wind; pleasures that draw half their substance from the presence of the friends who share them and are content with only a few shots or even with none at all; pleasures that would never come to us without the wild energy of our dogs – dogs that long only to hunt all day long and that seem unsatisfied unless their tongues are bleeding, unless their coats are spiked with gorse and caked all over with mud; and as you sit resting under the hedge at noon, they lie there with steaming coats and gaze at you in the hope of just two things: in the hope of a crust from your bread, and in their longing for more work in the afternoon – Oh! I have lost control of this sentence in the joy of it all, for there are so many joys to hunting pheasants that it is itself a joy, on a day toward the end of October, to realise that at last you are standing on the edge of them, that you loved the summer labour that leads up to them and are ready at last for the beginning of the sportsman's harvest.

I felt very happy as I looked down over my little kingdom; and the truth of it is that I also felt proud, proud that High Park is a place where pheasants are released with care and shot with reverence, a place where lunch is a dram and a sandwich under the sky, a place for a few friends to pursue common pleasures in each other's company, until at the end of it all, at the end of another day's sport, we walk down the meadow together with our dogs more or less at our sides, we walk down the meadow full of fresh memories of time spent in a beautiful place, with a dinner or two stowed in our game-

bags, full of fresh memories and brimful of praise. I hope that it will happen like this on Monday and on my other High Park days this season; a much larger hope is that it will continue to happen, both at High Park and in a thousand similar places, for years and years to come.

In the middle of all this pleasure and pride I have almost forgotten to tell you what it was that made this year's harvest festival a cause for special celebration. It concerns the land that runs along most of my southern boundary. There are about seventy acres of it and I learned a few days ago that my offer of a rental had been accepted and that I should be able shoot over it this season. This was the reason why the morning of my festival witnessed a ceremony that it has never seen before. It began with the building of a simple stile over the boundary fence. Then I climbed the stile, with just a hint of solemnity, and began a tour of my new ground. With the owner's permission I had, of course, been there before in order to assess the sporting potential of the land, but this was the first time I had walked his fields in the knowledge that before long I should be back there with a gun.

First I went down to the old plantation behind Low Park Pond and found that I liked what I saw. I liked the brambles beneath the old pines and the patches of gorse on the edge of them. I felt sure they would be sheltering a few pheasants when the time came to probe into their secrets with an eager spaniel. Then I crossed the flat boggy pasture that runs up to the edge of my meadow. What looked like an old cock scuttled away from my approach and a snipe sprang screeching into the sunlight. Crossing the sike I climbed the steep slope of the field that rises to meet the top of Beck Bank. There would be room for two guns here and, even if most of the birds that flew past them turned out to be too low for sport, there would be others that their presence would send back, flying high and fast to cross the guns waiting down in the meadow on the other side of the

sike. Beck Bank would no longer be a drive where I was forced to watch helplessly while my birds hopped over the boundary fence and ran for safety into fields where they could not be followed.

This was not the best of it. The best of it was a little further up, directly behind the old pen and almost on the top of the slope where, ever since I started releasing pheasants at High Park, I have eyed a long sprawl of gorse with a mixture of longing and resentment. It has always proved an irresistible draw to my pheasants. I know this because I have seen them running into it. I know it too because, before I reached my new agreement with the owner of this prime gorse covert, I had his permission to send dogs onto his land in search of wounded game. Merlin has often entered the gorse in search of a runner and, whenever Merlin has entered the gorse, hale and hearty pheasants have promptly clattered out of it. Sometimes there have been as many as a dozen of them, and I confess that last season, before Merlin was sent over my boundary with the smell of a wounded pheasant in his nostrils, I lined up my friends on my side of the fence, waiting with loaded guns for any birds that might break back towards the wood. I am not sure that this practice was altogether honourable, but in the future there will be no more pricks of guilt; instead of them there will be guns waiting on the far side of the gorse for those pheasants that continue to feel the pull of the South and head off for fields yet more distant from their hoppers and their home.

After gloating over this extensive and delectable spread of gorse I headed South myself: to two more patches of gorse growing down to a wall from the little ridge at the point where it forms the highest edge of the pasture. It seemed a long way up in the world; I was looking down over the top of Beck Bank and my meadow was down in the valley a long way beneath me. There was a bracing sense of space and elevation and here, I told myself, here up in the sunshine was a place that was likely to hold a few birds; they would

be good birds too if they flew over either of the guns that would be standing in the field below the wall. Walking on over the ridge I now came to the view for which I had been waiting so expectantly.

In front of me the land fell away sharply, but the ridge on which I was standing bent round to my left in the form of an eccentric amphitheatre. Towards the southern end of this imperfect half-circle a deep gully ran the full length of the slope, choked with gorse along its whole length and with wide extensions of gorse running out at the top. I shall describe it in greater detail when it has been part of a day's sport. Standing there on the morning of my Harvest Festival

and slowly following the long line of the gully with my eyes, I rejoiced in the sight of it; and I saw it not only as it was then, shining in soft October sunshine; I also saw it as it would be on some cold afternoon in December, with two or three guns lining the steep slope, with a biting wind blowing down the hill, and with pheasants rising from those high outgrowths of gorse and rising still higher as they followed the wind and swept over the guns.

The sight of the gully filled me with delight and expectation. I sat down for five minutes and smoked, thinking happily of the sport that the ground in front of me was surely going to produce. Then I went down to the bottom of the slope and walked up along the edge of the gorse. The gully itself was deeper than I remembered and the cover was thicker; it was bound to hold pheasants in dozens, especially once my own land had been shot a time or two. They would come to the Gully – note that it now has a capital letter – they would come to the Gully in search of peace and quiet and they would get a surprise. The Gully alone might add twenty birds to the season's bag. The big spread of gorse just over my boundary might do the same. The other bits and pieces could easily, between them, make it sixty. I began to think that in future seasons I should be needing at least two hundred poults; and that was before I came to the long rushy pasture that spreads on either side at the Gully's top, a pasture that could not fail to produce a few birds for walking guns.

I calmed down and forbade myself to jump to conclusions. I decided that the end of this season would be the time to decide how many birds I wanted to put down for the next. I also decided that on Monday, the day of my first shoot, we should leave all the new ground unvisited except for the gorse above the old pen. Perhaps a little outside day – or an outside afternoon – would be a good idea early in November, but I would not shoot my own land and my rented land on the same day until the first December shoot, which is always, you may remember, the occasion on which I attempt to produce something approaching a big bag. And there would be no hoppers hung anywhere over my boundaries this season; I should try to hold birds in the heart of the shoot. They would spread out naturally without grain to tempt them; hoppers in the Gully and other likely places would only encourage them to spread out too far.

I was absorbed in all this dreaming and planning when I suddenly bumped into my boundary fence and realised that my tour of inspection was over. I climbed the fence, thinking that I must put up some more stiles, and proceeded with the traditional ritual of my Harvest Festival. More than once, as I processed this way and that, sitting down here and there to smoke for a while and to look round at what was there to be seen; more than once, during my progress along the edges of my kingdom, my thoughts left the kingdom altogether, flying off to the Gully or the Old Pen Gorse and all the pheasants waiting to stream out of them on winter shooting days. It made my little autumn celebration an even deeper pleasure than it has always been in the past. At the end of it all I went home and, in obedience to established tradition, ate the only pheasant remaining from last season's harvest; with it, and for some time afterwards, I drank a bottle of burgundy; good burgundy, and I confess that I drank the lot of it, which was, or so it seemed at the time, almost demanded of me at the end of such a glorious day. There was no hangover in the morning and I resisted the temptation to walk over my rented land all over again.

As usual there were five of us, and we were the same five as usual. Four of our dogs were the same as well, but Toy's Bracken had died in the New Year and it was young Fern, a big black labrador, that was now prancing at his master's side. We met, as we always do, at ten o'clock and we did not hurry to start, for my ground can be covered in three or four hours; and it is delightful, at the beginning of a shooting day, especially at the beginning of the first day of the season, to stand and talk a while, drinking coffee and

picking up loose ends, making plans and wondering how the day will go and feeling how much sport there is stretching ahead of us over the next three months.

The day was cloudy and mild and still, very damp after the overnight rain, with near and misty horizons and with low cloud over the hills. The autumn trees glowed darkly as they dripped; and the earth, as we walked up the fields for the first little drive of a new season, oozed and squelched beneath our feet. We started with Beck Bank – we usually do – and, as I had expected, there were many pheasants lurking there in the brambles and the blackthorn and the matted tangles of rushy grass. Most of them ran from danger along the ditch that follows the line of my boundary fence. I could see them legging it up the slope and disappearing under the wire, while others used their wings to retreat in the same direction. The low cunning of these birds has always irritated me in the past; now it amused me, for I told myself that the next time it happened there might be guns waiting on the south side of the fence; and if my deserting pheasants were heading for the Old Pen Gorse or for the Gully, then one day before very long, they would be made to realise that their plan was not quite as clever as it might have seemed.

Not all the birds from Beck Bank took the coward's route to freedom. Perhaps half a dozen came over the three of us standing down by the sike, but most of them were low and were left to fly again; mine was the only shot, at a crossing hen which fell behind me on the edge of the Rise and was gathered by Merlin with all the wild energy of his youth. My shoot is the sort of shoot where a drive that produces a single bird can be counted a success; it is one of the pleasures of my sort of shoot. I should have preferred Beck Bank's only bird to have been shot by one of my friends rather than by me. Otherwise, given that it was the first drive of the season, it was an altogether satisfactory start to this year's harvest of pheasants.

It was a delightful day to be out under the sky. Sometimes there was a mist of warm drizzle, but never for more than a few minutes. Often the sky showed shadings of blue which hinted that before long we might be shooting in sunshine. There were one or two pelting showers and briefly there was the blessing of a rainbow over our heads. There was a sense of prelude to it all, if not of rehearsal, which is the essence of the season's first pheasant shoot: a shoot where you watch birds fly and think to yourself that they will fly better next time; a shoot where a big bag would be a blunder; a shoot that looks forward to deeper and colder pleasures that will come when the leaf is off the trees, when the year has turned to winter and the east wind is blowing snow down from the hills, and high pheasants over the sike, where my friends will be waiting for them with two stockings on each foot.

I am not going to bore you with a minute description of every drive. I was pleased with the Rise, for you may remember me telling you that I moved hoppers there in the hope of attracting and holding more birds. The dogs flushed at least twenty pheasants from the hedge-bottom and from the brashings to one side of the hedge. The cover down the slope of the Rise is not yet quite thick enough to hold squatting birds; it needs another year or two for the blackthorn to sprout and to spread, for the brambles to twist and tangle more extensively, for the aspens to spring up between every tubed tree, for the grass and the rushes to run still wilder and thicker riot. Give it a year or two and the Rise will have turned into a real rough shooter's covert; give it a year or two and the first shoot of the season may send forty, not twenty, pheasants streaming from the Rise.

This year we had to be content with twenty or so and, with no wind to turn them over the guns, most of them flew straight down the hedge and safely into the gorse. Perhaps a stop, or a flag-man, would persuade them to fly where they are meant to fly. I am not sure that flag-men and stops are really part of the scheme of things

87

at High Park, although I could punish or bribe a boy and see whether or not it works. Most of those twenty or so pheasants, anyway, did not cross the guns. Only one of them was shot, but this was a beautiful bird, a full-tailed hen that flew straight and high and then threw back its neck to Mick's shot before it fell in the long grass right on the edge of the sike.

There were very few birds up round the New Pen, but this was because the cover there was dripping wet. North Bank was full of pheasants, lurking in the gorse above the trees, and doubtless intending to stay there for an hour or two, until Merlin came along and suddenly changed their minds. The Penside was quieter than is usual for the first time through, but over my boundary the Old Pen Gorse held a good store of birds and confirmed its promise for shoots later in the season.

The birds flew very well for the first time of the season. I should not have been ashamed of them if it had been a month later and a day for undoubtedly serious sport. Of course some of them were low, which is always the case with early season birds; pheasants do not learn to love the sky until they have been up in it a time or two. Some of the birds were low, but there was no feeble flapping or fluttering; they flew with fast wing beats and with commendable speed, and there was barely a short tail to be seen at the back of them. They are fine birds and they will challenge us when they are stronger and more practised, especially when the wind blows.

One o'clock came and it was time to sit under the hedge by the meadow gate. I found that I had forgotten my lunch and, although I had not forgotten the whisky, I might as well have done, because Toy had also brought a whisky-filled flask and insisted that we should drink his rather than mine. In the event I ate more than I had planned to bring for myself, begging a sandwich from Phil and another from Mick and a pie from one or the other of them. Then

Austin, deciding that it was his turn to be generous to his host, presented me with a half-rotten banana. I love bananas when the skin has turned black, and the sandwiches were far better than those that I make. I tend to think of my health and fill my bread with tomatoes and tuna shavings, whereas what you really want for a lunchtime shooting sandwich is pork brawn and slabs of beef; this is what I learned from leaving my own lunch behind and I think that, in future at High Park, I shall expect my guests to provide me with my piece. It will become a tradition of the place and they will vie for my favour with pork brawn and slabs of beef, also with smoked salmon and foie gras and cold haunches of venison. I most certainly approve of Irish whiskey as our lunchtime tipple on a shooting day. This too will turn into a High Park feature, with a choice of Jamieson's and the Paddy and with a bottle of Bushmills for those who insist upon protestant liquor.

Merlin had been something of a worry to me in the days before the shoot. I was afraid that the rough cover that makes High Park a young spaniel's heaven might prove too much for his ageing and arthritic joints. I need not have bothered myself, for he showed all his old relish for the thickest tangles of the stuff and was ready for more of it at the end of the day. He was as stiff as a board the next morning and could barely hobble down the stairs, but by lunchtime he had more or less recovered and made a show of bounding through the woods where I took him for exercise in the afternoon.

The day's bag was just about right for the first day at High Park; there were nine pheasants and one rabbit (I could have done with a few more of them) and there was a very expensive crow. Everyone had a few shots and everyone killed a pheasant. I killed two with three shots and fired two more at rabbits that kept running. We finished at three o'clock and talked over the day for ten minutes at the meadow gate. Then it was down the fields and back to the vehicles, though for me there was a brief diversion to scatter a

bucket of grain on Low Park Pond. I confess that I was still feeling predatory; it may have been those two missed rabbits coming right at the end of the afternoon's sport; whatever it was I was keen to end with a successful shot and so, on the chance of finding duck on the pond – a remote prospect, I suppose, after a morning and afternoon of sporadic gunfire – on the chance, anyway, of surprising a mallard or two on Low Park Pond, I loaded each barrel of my gun with a bismuth cartridge from my top pocket, I left the bucket of grain well back in the field and crept up towards the water. No duck sprang into the sky, but a crow flapped away from the edge of the pond, which is why one ended up in the bag and why he was an expensive crow.

I shall not shoot my own ground again until the middle of November, when time comes round for the boys' shoot; but in just under a fortnight I shall try an outside afternoon on the Villa Park land; which, by the way, is what my rented fields call themselves and there are so many parks of various sorts in my neck of the woods that it is all rather confusing. It is also inappropriate, because neither High Park nor Low Park nor Villa Park, with their steep and rushy fields, with their dry stone walls and their rusty fences, with their sprawling masses of gorse and their unkempt hedges and their untidy patches of woodland, because all of it, apart from the really wild bits, is rough grazing or old hayfields on the edge of the moors; and because none of it conforms to my idea of what parkland should look like, with a sculptured lake or two and a few temples and a tasteful spacing of stately trees. The Villa Park outside afternoon, anyway, will be Digby's turn and, in spite of that, I am already looking forward to it.

OCTOBER

On my way back from High Park, at the end of shooting days or on days when I have been out there just to fill hoppers and to take a look at things, I often stop the Land Rover by a roadside stile. Then I cross the limestone wall and walk down the field with a bucket of grain; a rabbit or two usually scampers from patches of dying thistles for the shelter of its warren in the walled spinney below me on the right; always the sheep rush up to mob the bucket in the hope of a distribution, while, unless there is mist on the hills, the sharp outline of Wild Boar Fell lift themselves calmly above us all, above me and the startled rabbits and the greedy Swaledale sheep.

It is a sloping field and, at the bottom of the slope, beneath the cross wall perhaps twenty yards from the spinney, there is a hollow of marshy ground that is usually no more than an muddy squelch in the summer; some summers it has been more like a dustbowl than a wet place but, whatever it is like during the summer, with the coming of the autumn rains it turns into a pond; it is always a shallow pond with clumps of rushes sticking out of the water; I scatter my corn all over it, knowing that not a single grain will be too deep for the duck. It is also a secret pond; you could stand almost anywhere in the surrounding pastures without knowing that it was there. The mallard, together with an occasional teal, favour this pond for its shallowness; I favour it because the duck are fond of it and because it is a lovely and a secret place.

I have flighted this secret little pond for years, never leaving it with more than three or four duck in my bag, sometimes leaving it with nothing at all, but almost always feeling grateful for the time I have spent crouching in the angle of the wall that runs down virtually to the edge of the water. And, either before or after flight, there is usually a cup of tea in the farmhouse to which the pond belongs; more often than not there is cake as well as tea – once or twice I have taken a whole cake back with me to Sedbergh – and sometimes the whisky bottle has appeared on the table instead of the tea pot.

There is a convivial aspect to flighting this pond which is a special part of the pleasure of going there.

On the last day of October I sat in the angle of the wall for the first time this season. I had fed the pond the day before and was encouraged to find that all the corn had already gone. There was nothing of the dying glory that often fills the sky as we duck shooters sit waiting for the sound of wings. It was an evening of cloud and drizzle, with a damp, sagging greyness that turned very slowly both greyer and damper. Crows on their way to roost seemed like black patches flapping through the grey air. A grey heron creaked down to the water, lifting off again with a laboured beating of grey wings when Merlin snorted with inappropriate excitement.

I sat there on my bucket, watching drops of water gather and fall from the dead tips of the thistle-stalks all around me. I was thinking of past evenings by the pond: of how Merlin used to leap the high wall behind us to gather any duck that had fallen in the field on its other side. I told myself that now he would need the gate; and then I remembered a September evening when a mallard had flown between me and the moon and had fallen through the silver air with such compelling grace that, filled with wonder, I sent Merlin over the wall to collect my bird and then put my gun in its sleeve, happy just to sit there smoking for a while before getting up to leave.

There was nothing quite so memorable the other night, although there were more duck than I have sometimes seen flying into my secret pond. On rare occasions I have seen nothing at all; but on this occasion, as the grey light thickened to darkness, a single mallard came over high and fell to my shot. I kept Merlin by me because the bird had fallen on the wrong side of the wall and I did not want the old spaniel scrambling over it with his gammy joints (my leg, by the way, seems to have mended itself; there have been no aches or twinges for more than a week). Very soon the rhythm of wings was throbbing through the damp air again and suddenly the air above the water was full of duck-shapes planing down towards the pond. They were easy birds, but I am not used to seeing more than a dozen mallard together in the sky above me. I hesitated in my choice of a target, bungled the shot and was left with a cartridge in my barrel and nothing at which to shoot it.

But this was only for a second. A pair of duck must have settled in the field close to the water; when coming into small ponds they often do this and then waddle a few yards before settling down to feed. Anyway, the shot at one of the big pack put them in the air and the second barrel put one of them back on the ground. Merlin was sent to retrieve and was barely back with a drake mallard in his mouth when another and even bigger party of duck-shapes suddenly descended from the sky. Again I fluffed the first barrel but this time I was quicker with the second and dropped a departing bird before it was out of range. Merlin did his job in a matter of seconds; then I sent him through the gate to find my first bird and, with this stowed in the game bag, it was back to the farmhouse for a cup of tea and a slice of chocolate cake. The whisky bottle stayed in the cupboard. It was half-term and so there was no Tuesday Club; but there was a glass of fino while I wrote up my game-book and there was half a bottle of Crozes-Hermitage to go with the steak. It was a rich and warm and satisfying wine and it was very good to drink after so grey, so damp and so satisfying a flight.

CHAPTER FIVE

NOVEMBER

The boy's shoot; bad Digby; the benefits of
fieldsports for professionals; nine birds in
an afternoon; favourite days in the shooting
season; ferreting; a glimpse of the Lunesdale
hunt; man's relationship with animals

There were only three of us; there was big Jamie and little Jamie and I, with bad Digby in attendance to hunt and gather for us. It was one o'clock in the afternoon. Morning school had finished just over half an hour an ago; we had reached High Park, we had eaten our pies in the Land Rover and now we were ready to start. There was a sharp wind and a bright sky and the rising fields shone all round us. Most of the trees were bare, though shrubby willows and the hazels along the hedges were still clinging to a faded scatter of yellow. It was an early November afternoon on the edge of winter; to be going shooting seemed the natural response to the weather and the season, especially after a morning spent in a classroom; but for me, as well as this familiar sense of release and exhilaration, there was a feeling of special expectancy, which was because, for the first time, I was

about to explore the land over my boundary in the company of a gun and a spaniel. It was the beginning of my outside afternoon.

Try to remember the Gully as I described it to you in the account of my Harvest Festival. Recall how it runs down, right down, the steep slope of a long pasture, choked with gorse and brambles along its whole course and with a trickle of water running along its bed. There are a few hawthorns and rowans rising out of the gorse. Towards the top of the slope a fence runs across the Gully, dividing the greater part of its length from its beginnings in the field above. Along the line of this fence stand four tall and leafless beech trees. Their trunks are shining silver in the pale sunshine and, beyond them, I am standing on the edge of the gorse, which reaches out from the top of the Gully in long fingers and spreading patches. I am standing there in the sunshine with Digby on a lead, waiting, just as soon as both Jamies have got themselves into position, to release my wilful spaniel into a wilful spaniel's idea of paradise.

The boys have already shot two rabbits and a pheasant, while I have learned that birds in those two patches of gorse right up on the ridge of the field fly where I was hoping they would fly, which is over the wall and towards Beck Bank, rising all the time and curling on the wind. I am still wondering why, a few minutes ago, I put neither of the Jamies over the wall in order to intercept the birds on their way back to my land. Perhaps I was impatient to get to where I am standing now. It is not a mistake, anyway, that will be made the next time we do the patches.

For the manoeuvre just about to begin, I have placed both Jamies on the same side of the Gully – the right side looking down – expecting flushed birds to swing over them as they head back towards their home. If they rise as they fly and curl away from the dropping line of the Gully they will be wonderful birds. I shall be on the other side, trying to control bad Digby and hoping to deal with any pheasants that break out in my direction.

Almost as soon as Digby is released from his lead and rushes into the gorse, a hen pheasant takes noisily to the wing, flying straight out to one side and falling to my shot. Digby then retrieves it in Digby's way, which means dropping it five yards away from his master (there is, of course, the variation in which he stands five yards from his master without dropping the bird and with no intention whatsoever of doing so until his master has walked up to him and pulled him fairly sharply by the ear).

Back in the Gully Digby flushes another pheasant, which flies fast and high and full of sunshine towards the higher Jamie, but too wide of him for an effective shot. I tear my breeches while clambering over the fence; Digby goes under the wire and almost immediately – and briefly – impresses me; for, although the higher Jamie missed that wide pheasant, he has already killed two fleeing rabbits and both of them have tumbled into the gorse. Digby now proceeds to extract them in almost exemplary fashion, bringing them both within inches of my outstretched hand, before disappearing back into the gorse and continuing to ignore my whistle.

There are more birds in the Gully, but they do not behave quite as I had hoped; a hen decides that the best route to safety is uphill rather than down, offering me an easy going away shot. This hen is the beginning of a theory that will need testing in the further course of the season. It concerns gorse, as most things do on my shoot, and my theory is that, gorse being such thick and tangled and intractable stuff, it is much more difficult to predict the way that birds will fly from it than from most other sorts of cover. It is, I suppose, one of the excitements of gorse, and perhaps next time we do those patches up on the ridge, with guns in position ready for pheasants flushing over the wall, perhaps next time half a dozen birds will find their

escape from the uphill edge of the gorse where there will be no-one waiting for them.

Bad Digby, anyway, found the gorse in the Gully very exciting indeed. Right from the bottom he produced a final surprise; it was a cock bird that rose very steeply into the sunshine and then collapsed with a splash onto the sodden earth. I felt a twinge of conscience, for I knew that my shot had killed it the split second before big Jamie's rang out. It was no more than a twinge and it had almost gone by the time the old cock had been gathered.

Digby had put four birds out of the Gully; I suppose I had been hoping for more, but three of them had been shot and I was confident the drive would be more productive when we came there a month later. I was wondering where to work the dog next – if that is the appropriate verb for my ineffective management of bad Digby – working him in the hope of finding a bird or two for the boys before it was time to finish.

But first it was time to set a bad example, for it was warm in the field bottom and the game bags were heavy. I declared a five-minute rest before the trudge back uphill. I spent a small portion of it, with at least a show of sincerity, apologising to big Jamie for shooting his bird; I spent more of it looking back at the Gully and the bold rise of the land, at the bright fields and the shining splashes of water still left from the heavy rain of the day before; I also outlined my rough plan for the last half hour or so of our sport; and then, in the middle of it all, I did what schoolmasters are not meant to do nowadays. I struck a sinful match and smoked some part of a disgraceful pipeful of tobacco: all done, you will realise with a gasp of horror, in front of impressionable pupils and done moreover without the faintest stirrings of shame or the slightest prick of guilt. I am undoubtedly a very poor role-model for the young.

In spite of this noxious inhalation of smoke I made it back up the hill without a heart attack or the sudden onset of bronchitis or even a minor coughing fit. Digby then bounded along muddy ditch bottoms and through a wide rushy pasture. He flushed five or six birds, but he pushed too far ahead and most of them rose well out of range. Two were within shot and just one of them fell. By now there were long shadows creeping out from the walls; the folds and undulations of every field were marked out by bold patterns of shade and sunlight, telling us that it was time to leave my pheasants in peace, time to walk down the pastures in the slanting light, with five pheasants and four rabbits making up the bag for our outside afternoon. I was delighted with this first shooting excursion over the boundary fence and I was already looking forward to the next one; and it was this next one, early in December, that I was expecting to

produce a big show of birds, for then my own land would have been shot in the morning, sending pheasants rushing for shelter into the gorse and the rushes and the ditches where we had just found our afternoon's sport.

Before we left I sent the Jamies up the meadow to fill two buckets of grain for the flight pond, while I got out my pipe again and sat waiting by the sike. The wind had dropped away by now; the air was still and the last light was in the tops of the trees on Beck Bank, in the tapering firs and the orange larches and the golden beeches. Beneath this brightness the shadows had already merged and the darkness was gathering. The water murmured and splashed. Digger's caked and matted coat steamed on the air; and, though the afternoon had felt like the beginning of winter, here, where the sheltered trees carried more leaf, with the evening calm now settled over the land and with that transfiguring light in the high branches, here it was still autumn, hushed and serene and very beautiful.

I am sure there come to all of us similar moments of complete contentment when, at the end of a few hours' or a whole day's sport, with a few pheasants or a few rabbits stowed in our bags, we sit in contemplation of the landscape that enriches us in so many ways. And we know then, as we look at the light in the branches and at the climbing darkness beneath them, as we listen to the sound of the water and light our pipes and mutter a few words to our muddied and weary spaniels, at such moments we know that we are not cruel men addicted to guilty pleasures; we know that our love of shooting is a natural and wholesome love, because it could never, were it a brutal and corrupting passion, bring this mood of such deep and such numinous peace. On my outside afternoon, by the way, just to keep you up to date with the statistics of my performance this season, I fired five cartridges and shot three pheasants and a rabbit. It was, for some reason, the rabbit that pleased me most of all.

I have said that I prefer flighting duck alone, and what I have said is true; but it would be selfish never to share the delights of your favourite flight pond with anyone else, and so, last Tuesday evening, after Low Park Pond had been rested for a few weeks – three of them, in fact, rather than the four to which I bound myself at the end of my last flight there – and when its puddled and feathered margins persuaded me that the time had come round for another damp hour sitting on a bucket beneath the old crab apple tree, I went there with a friend and waited to see what the failing light would bring in.

As it happened few duck came, for the air thickened to mist almost as soon as we were settled on our buckets. Doubtless the mallard that were planning to eat their dinners on Low Park Pond delayed their departure from the tarns and rivers where they had dabbled the day away; doubtless they flew in for their food after darkness, once the mist cleared and the stars shone out. I think I should have left with the mist if I had been by myself. But it does not matter that I stayed; our few shots can have caused little disturbance and I may flight again in a fortnight as long as the corn is being taken.

I did not leave because I knew that my friend was keen to stay. I sat there by the water with the pale shapes of things all round me. The old heron flapped past, looking gaunter and greyer and more ghostly than usual. My pheasants were particularly noisy and two of them went up to roost in the pines behind us, so that for ten minutes the thick air was full of their shouting and the flapping of their wings. The misty air seemed to stir the lust of a tup that was sharing the field with us and with his harem. He was a texel (I had spotted this before the mist came down) and he was every bit as ugly as the rest of his kind; he looked like a cross between a sheep and a pig, incorporating the least attractive features of both animals; there was a look of debauched concupiscence about him; he looked like a tup with a fatty liver and an inordinate sex drive. Perhaps, in spite of appearances, he is a bashful and considerate tup; perhaps, respecting the modesty of his ewes, he always waits for the shades of evening before making his first advance; perhaps he only makes love on evenings shrouded in mist. Anyway, as I sat on my bucket, waiting for the duck and smoking my pipe, the murky silhouette of him made it plain to me that he was at last vigorously employed.

The tup moved on over the brow in search of further conquests, while I sat there on my bucket waiting for the duck, pondering my bachelor existence and looking forward to the boys' shoot on the coming Saturday. I wondered when would be the right time to flight the secret pond again and decided that, since I had forgotten to feed it since I shot there on the last day of October, the right time would be at least a month away. My thoughts drifted away from shooting and I asked myself – already knowing the answer – whether I agreed with one or two of my colleagues who clearly think that LWC spends too much time sitting by duck ponds when he should be sitting at his desk and producing action plans for the department that he is supposed to run; and doubtless they also think that he goes off fishing, or disappears to feed his pheasants when he should be settling down to spend the afternoon writing schemes of work, whatever they are, for the next five years. And what about inventing minutes for all those meetings that the modern head of department is expected to convene? We had a meeting once and it seemed a complete waste of time. I think that I would rather invent a few pages of minutes than hold another one.

Going shooting and fishing is much more useful for a school-master than devoting himself to schemes of work and minutes and action plans: this was the answer that I already knew, for I knew that I never work more happily or more productively than on return from an afternoon's shooting or while looking forward to an evening flight, unless it is on Sunday evenings in the summer term when, after spending the best part of the day by the Eden or the Wharfe, I feel so full of contentment that marking a set of Latin sentences seems a rare privilege, whereas reading Horace or Virgil in preparation for Monday's lessons is undoubtedly the perfect complement to those wonderful hours passed along the margins of running water.

Were I a headmaster, which (except in my worst nightmares) I never shall be, I should encourage all my underlings to fish and to shoot, and I dare say that most of the men I appointed would be devoted to at least one of our fieldsports. I should fill my school with fishing and shooting and hunting folk; it would mean that we had something to talk about other than the next school inspection or the prospects for the first fifteen next Saturday; but I should also adopt this novel practice in the sincere conviction that the time my staff spent outdoors would return them to their classrooms both invigorated and enlarged. And, for the same reason, all headmasters should go fishing at least once a week during the trout season, turning to sport with duck and pheasants once the Christmas term comes round again. It should be written into their contracts.

It was damp on my bucket and it seemed that no duck were going to appear. I began to plan a sporting programme for Mr Blair, a plan designed to turn him into a better prime minister. Trout fishing was at the heart of it, but there were August visits to the moors and there were evenings on a bucket as my guest at Low Park Pond. There were afternoons spent filling hoppers, with Mr Blair fighting his way up muddy slopes and sliding back down them and learning to love the colour of the treacherous and sustaining earth. There was the reward for all this hard work, with spaniel days along frosty hedges, bringing a few rabbits and a pheasant or two for Cherie's larder. There were one or two proper driven days, but it was mostly humble stuff; and I knew that, at the end of all these fishing and shooting days, Mr Blair would return to Downing Street with

such peace inside him, and with such visionary memories of beautiful places, that he would see things clearly and judge things wisely and think warm thoughts about hunting people.

I was so involved with my scheme to reform Mr Blair that the first duck took me by surprise; there was only one shot and it was way behind its target. When the next bird came I had forgotten about the prime minister, unless it was his lingering influence that misguided my first barrel; the second, at any rate, brought a fine drake to earth. Meanwhile my friend, undistracted by thoughts of headmasters and designs to turn jobbing politicians into statesmen, saw the few duck that flew through the mist much sooner than I; and he shot straight and killed three birds with four shots. But soon it was time to leave Low Park Pond to the tup and his harem, to the white mist and the hooting owls, to the pheasants trying to get a night's sleep in the old pines behind us, to these and to all the wandering creatures of the night. I hope there were not too many foxes among them.

They would not celebrate the sort of bag my Boys' Shoot brought at the sort of shoot where pheasants cross the line in thousands and where hundreds fall to earth on a single drive. There was no need for double guns and loaders the other Saturday afternoon at High Park; we did not need a team of pickers-up to collect the dead and the wounded at the end of every drive. But on some of them, where pheasants came more thickly than they have ever come before, on some of my little drives one or two of my young shooters killed as many as three birds at a single stand, with perhaps a bird or two missed as well. Now three birds to a single gun in the course of a single drive is the sort of sport we dream of at High Park. It does

not often come true. And we do not expect a day without a blank drive, and, in order to bring the bag somewhere near double figures, we normally finish the day by walking the top fields in the hope of a last bird or two from the rushes.

There was no need for this the other Saturday. There were pheasants in the sky from the start of things and they were pheasants that knew how to fly. They would have flown even faster if the afternoon had not been so soft and so still; for the November weather, which had seemed a week earlier to be thinking that it was time for winter, time for sharp winds and the first frosty nights, had decided that it preferred autumn after all, that it liked to see midges dancing on the warm air, and that it preferred trees with some coloured remnants of foliage still hanging from their branches. The weather had decided that, down in the shelter of the sike, those few birches that still carried a full head of golden leaves were far too beautiful to sacrifice just yet to the ravages of rough winds and freezing air.

It was a still, damp day, but it did not transmit its mood to my birds. They did not amble on their way through the sky. They rose with a clatter of wings; they knew at once where they were going and they got on with it. Those that crossed the sike were high and fast and the boys did well to bring so many of them down. They did better still on the first drive for, although there were some challenging birds from Beck Bank, there were others that flew down the slope and crossed the line very low. They would have been easy going-away shots but, thinking that they would also have been have been unworthy shots, the boys left them well alone; which only doubled my shame late in the afternoon when, realising that a record bag was in prospect, I promptly secured it by killing a pheasant that should still be a living one. Its death was also a broken promise and I shall come back to it before I finish with this record of my boys' shoot.

Old Merlin was disobedient but at the same time he was beyond praise. He rushed into the gorse just as in the days of his prime, and he stayed in it, in the thickest and sharpest and deepest parts of it, until he was satisfied that he was alone there with no more pheasants for company. Sometimes he plunged in again, just to make certain that his job had been properly done. There were times when I lost all sense of contact with him, guessing his whereabouts from the rise of a bird or from sudden and snorting agitation in bushes fifty or sixty yards away from me. The notes of my whistle rarely acted as a means of control; they were more like a sort of musical accompaniment to the afternoon's sport, unless perhaps they were an encouragement to my Merlin to forget all about his master for the time being and get on with the work that he loves so dearly. They seemed to raise his spirits rather than to rein them in; and his enthusiasm was undiminished at the end of the afternoon. He did not want to leave High Park and it was only in the evening that he remembered his age and his joints; for he would rather not have moved when my claret was finished and it was time for him to hobble out under the stars for a few minutes before going to sleep again.

Throughout the afternoon – there were lessons in the morning and we could not start until one o'clock – the bag mounted steadily. Beck Bank brought half a dozen birds, the Rise a single cock. There were pheasants all along the Penside, and they were the best birds of the day, rising above the trees and then rushing over the guns waiting way below them on the edge of the sike. They were fine birds and nine of them were killed. North Bank added four birds to the bag, one of which was my pheasant of shame, for it was a low bird and it was by no stretch of the imagination a fast bird. It briefly tarnished the glory of the record bag that came with its fall; for, as soon as it had been shot, I remembered that I had vowed never again to help myself to an easy pheasant on my own shoot – elsewhere I do not feel the temptation – just to add another digit to the day's

entry in my game-book, just to creep another pheasant nearer a total for the season that will convince me that it has all been worthwhile. Undoubtedly I am a weak and sinful man.

Perhaps this lapse of mine should have spoiled my day. I confess that it did not. Two birds were killed from the Gutter, just one from the Whins, though a runner came down near the old pen but was never found. It was, I think, the only ungathered bird. At High Park the second shoot of the season is always likely, in terms of the size of the bag, to be the one of the best shoots of the season. It was so last year, when nineteen pheasants were brought back to the Land Rover at the end of the day. This season we carried twenty three down the meadow as the light began to thicken. All but one of them had been fine and sporting birds. In forgiving myself for an action that ill became a man on the edge of his half-century of years, I swore that it would never happen again, and then fell to wondering whether I should celebrate High Park's bounty with claret or with burgundy.

It was claret in the end, and it was not grand claret; it was the sort of claret that complements an afternoon spent in the open air on a little shoot that covers little more than fifty acres. It was not grand claret but it was rich and satisfying and, when Merlin had been out for his starlit hobble and was back snoring under his master's desk, his master found that there was just time for a small whisky before his own bedtime came along.

Sometimes I wonder which days of the shooting season I like best: those days that bring the beauty and the excitement of sport, days when pheasants are pushed into the sky, when shots ring out and birds fall or fly on, days when Merlin believes for a time that heaven

has come down to earth; or those days between shoots when I trudge from hopper to hopper, when there is time to savour small sights and sniff the smell of rotting leaves, when the mewing of a buzzard or the obstreperous crowing of a cock pheasant counts for a loud sound, when there is no high challenge up there in the sky, no expectancy charging the air, only soft contentment and the silent flutter of falling leaves, and to all my slow activity there is the soothing accompaniment of water running over the stones, and everywhere round me there is the peace that belongs to quiet and lonely places.

Two days after my boys' shoot I found that my afternoon was free, which in summer means rivers; at this time of the year it usually means High Park, and I was there by half past two. It was a cold and a bright day with no wind; already the land was lying in

that afternoon slant of light that makes beautiful places look twice as beautiful, seaming them with lines and stripes and ridges of shadow between the stretched brightness of the sun. The old heron was on the edge of Low Park Pond (it is impossible to look at a heron and think of youth; he may be a bird of one or two summers but the long beak and the gaunt shape and the grey colour force you to think of him as old). This afternoon, anyway, the heron on the edge of Low Park Pond gleamed blue and silver, as well as grey, in the low light; he was as stiff and as still as ice and his beak was pointing sharply to the sky. There were moving flocks of fieldfares along the hedges; the steel in their feathers was very clear; and the neat lines of molehills running up the meadow were already throwing little shadows ahead of them as I walked past them on my way to the meadow gate.

I had come to make sure that there was plenty of grain in the hoppers, although it was really no more than an excuse, because on Thursday there would be boys with me to carry sacks and buckets and do all the heavy work. I had come because I wanted to be there, and because, after every shoot, I am always keen to get out to High Park as soon as possible, just to reassure myself that the recent disturbance has not persuaded all my surviving birds that life would be more peaceful somewhere else. Wandering here and there I came across clumps of feathers. Each fresh sight of them brought the brief fear of a fox, until I remembered that those feathers under the birches, or on the edge of the gorse, or half way up Pheasant Hill, marked the spot where a bird had fallen on Saturday, or that two or three gathered birds had been left down by the sike where I now found the signs of them. I even came across some reminders of the deed of shame that had secured Saturday's record bag. I stood by those wet tufts of feather for a moment and hung my head in guilty recollection, but it was only for a moment and I was soon on my way again cheerfully enough.

It was difficult not to be cheerful for, though there were these memorials of the dead, my land was also full of living pheasants with long tails. They scuttled into cover and the retreating cocks glowed in the long fingers of sunshine that were poking through the trees; and, above the hopper furthest from the meadow gate, there was a red squirrel dangling from a branch and making noises at me, until suddenly he took fright and was bounding away through the tops of the trees.

There were less pleasing sights, though there were no mangled pheasant carcasses to be seen, no tattered bits of wing, no bones still adorned with a few torn remnants of flesh, no headless corpses; but on the edge of the gorse and again up on the open ground above the old pen my eye caught the slimy gleam of fresh fox droppings. I told myself that, by mid-November, only witless or weak or wounded pheasants were likely prey for a prowling fox; and anyway there were plenty of rabbits to keep my prowler happy, both healthy rabbits and those pitiful creatures with puffy and closed eyes, one of which I had considerately banged on the head on my way up the meadow.

The floor of the wood was yellow with the autumn's last fall of leaves; the bed of the sike was starred with them, shining through the brown water. I went up to the new pen and filled the hoppers still hanging there, thinking that I should perhaps move one more of them down into the gorse or into the main wood. I began to look forward to my next shoot on the first Saturday of December, when I plan to do my own ground in the morning and then my rented land in the afternoon, the hope being that the morning's sport will push birds into the Gully, into the patches of gorse above the wall and into the rushy pasture that spreads out on either side from the top of the Gully. I thought that something like twenty pheasants would be a pleasing bag for this first December shoot, unless frost sets in and brings birds rushing back to my hoppers. A week of hard weather

might work wonders; it might even bring another High Park record; and it might bring woodcock from further East, adding variety to our sport and demanding, on the night of their eating, the high honour of burgundy as the only fitting tribute to the richness of their flesh.

I looked ahead to the next day when gunfire would resound over my little valley, but I was very happy with the present, and with the prospect of the intervening visits that I would spend wandering with buckets of grain through damp afternoons or through level winter sunshine, feeding my birds and relishing the sight of them and enjoying the quietness of it all. Returning to the sike I walked down into a land of shadow, but all round me there was still light high in the trees and on the bank tops: pale and lingering light that made the intricately meshed patterns of the branches very sharp and dark and clear. It was light that seemed somehow to be coming from below, slanting up out of the earth with its lower edge creeping very gradually towards the tips of the highest larches and the tallest firs. I sat by the meadow gate and smoked for a few minutes, watching a rabbit lollop out into the grass and listening to my birds as they began to think aloud about going up to roost.

I cannot remember what I thought about myself, except that, with pheasants now preparing themselves for their perches in the trees, it was time for me to get up and walk down the meadow. But I sat there a few minutes longer, and I suppose I was telling myself, among other things, that still winter evenings are very beautiful, and that I loved High Park just as much for the pleasure of sitting in the shadows while the sun sets as for the more impetuous pleasures that belong to shooting days. I know that I was very thankful to be there, consciously or perhaps unwittingly acknowledging that these very different pleasures feed on each other and between them make up all the wonderful richness of our sport. Very soon it was time to leave.

In certain conditions I am very fond of a few hours' ferreting, although I must confess at once that I am not over fond of ferrets. It would be different, I suppose, had I spent a childhood surrounded by ferrets and if I had grown to love them from my earliest years; but, as far as ferrets are concerned, I belonged to a deprived family and, doubtless because of this, I can never look at them without thinking of their teeth and how sharp they are, and how prone these same teeth are to remain firmly locked together once they have penetrated flesh. I can never look at ferrets without thinking of weasels and stoats, and so I can never persuade myself that, deep down, they are not vicious creatures; or that, given half a chance, they would pass up the opportunity to bite the hand that feeds and fondles them. I know that properly brought-up ferrets are affectionate beasts; I know that my mistrust of the whole race is unfair and unreasonable; I know that my attitude to ferrets will shock those thousands of devoted ferret-keepers who dote on the little creatures and expect to hear nothing but praise of their gentle habits and their winning ways. All I can do is to beg the forgiveness of all ferret-lovers, to assure them that their high opinion of the ferret character is undoubtedly the correct opinion, at the same time asking them to dismiss the foibles of a foolish and ignorant man as so much stuff and nonsense.

I do not think that I could ever learn to love ferrets; my fear of their teeth is too deeply ingrained: which means that, for me, the first condition of enjoyable ferreting is that somebody else handles the ferrets, while I stand nearby smoking a pipe and looking suitably rustic with a gun over my shoulder. The second is that the ferrets are of the sort that do not disappear down a rabbit-hole and then decide to stay there, only blinking up at the light of day again once spades have been energetically delving the hard and rooty earth for at least half an hour. Ferreting with ferrets of this tendency is very tedious and not worth the time or all that effort with the spade.

And I do not like ferreting in hard weather. Standing on the edge of a bury while the wind blows with ice on its breath and while rabbits refuse to bolt is far too cold for comfort; and, when at last a rabbit does decide to head for a part of the world that he will not have to share with an enemy bent on slaughter, then the odds are that my frozen thumb will be so slow on the safety catch that he will have found shelter in a ferretless hole long before I have managed to pull the trigger.

There are many sorts of day when I should prefer most forms of human activity to going ferreting; there are many ferrets with whom I should never choose to share an afternoon's sport; but give me a friend with three or four ferrets that pop down holes and then pop out again as soon as their work is done (there really are ferrets of this sort); then give me a soft day in November, a day when my pheasants need resting for at least another three weeks before they are forced onto the wing again, a day when I cannot think of another flight for at least a fortnight; give me the afternoon to spare and let my thoughts turn themselves to the prospect of some sport with the gun; give me all this and I shall probably go in search of my friend to suggest that he should put his ferrets in a box and head out with me to some of those buries on the edge of my rented ground, to see if we can find some amusement for a few hours and go home at the end of it all with a supper or two in our bags.

You need rabbits, of course, for successful ferreting, which was all that bothered me the other afternoon as a friend and I and a box of ferrets trudged over the wet earth to begin our investigations in the little warren on the bank above Low Park Pond. I was bothered because, all through the autumn, we have come across sick rabbits as well as healthy ones. Whenever I have been out at High Park in recent weeks, I have seen some of those sad rabbits with blind eyes and faltering hops; there have been many more of them in the last few weeks and there have also been many more carcasses scattered

through the fields. It surprises me that the buzzards are not too fat to fly; it saddens me to see the signs of death and disease all over my land, although the same signs bring carrion comfort in the hope that the foxes of Stainmore will feast on helpless rabbit-flesh and leave my pheasants alone. But stricken rabbits are a pitiful sight; whatever benefits their sickly presence may bring to me as a preserver and shooter of game, I should prefer to be without them; and a ferreter, of course, even a very occasional one like me, hates every appearance of the hideous disease that can wipe out his sport in the course of a few short weeks.

It was this that bothered me as I waited with my gun on the bank above Low Park Pond; I could not help wondering how many healthy rabbits were waiting for us down the holes. And would the ferrets kill a sick one and glut themselves and then close their eyes in the comfortable darkness, sleeping the afternoon away until our sweat and our spades invaded their peace. I need not have bothered, for the afternoon turned into one of the best that I have ever spent in the company of a gun and somebody else's ferrets.

From every bury the ferrets – and they were exemplary speci-mens of their kind – from every bury the ferrets expelled a rabbit or two; from some of the bigger warrens as many as a dozen rabbits fled into the light. And bolted rabbits offer the guns waiting for them plenty of variety. Some rabbits take their time about it; they are evicted with their dignity almost intact and, though they look easy targets, I often miss them. Others, with no concern for appear-ances, regard speed as of the essence; they erupt from their holes and to knock them over with a charge of shot is no small challenge. Some dart from one hole to the next; others head for the open spaces.

Some rabbits run straight down slopes, others scamper across them, while some prefer an uphill route to safety. Often they appear unannounced; sometimes they inform you, with an underground squeal or with a succession of subterranean thumps, that they are considering a change of air.

It is fine sport, ferreting is, as long as the ferrets know their business and the rabbits are in the mood to bolt. It is unpredictable and exciting and it is amusing to watch ferrets going about their work. They never seem in a hurry; they often seem bored or bemused as they hesitate on the lip of a hole; they seem uncertain what they are meant to be doing, unsure of their purpose in life or perhaps just disinclined to go to the trouble of sniffing their way down yet another dark passage. And always, when at last they shuffle back blinking into the light, always they seem completely unaware of all the panic they have been spreading down there in the darkness; they seem like ambling and incompetent predators with no passion for their work; but they are, of course, not at all what they seem.

It can be fine sport, ferreting can; the other day it was as fine as my limited experience has ever known it. The air was dank and mild and it was pleasant standing under the grey clouds and waiting for the next rabbit to appear. There were rabbits from the bank above Low Park Pond; there were rabbits from the hedge-bottom along the sides of the field. Three buzzards were in the sky, mewing as though in anger that we were taking for sport what they depend upon for food. Up on my rented ground there are some small buries along the line of the wall that drops down to the marshy land at the bottom of the Gully; there were three or four rabbits here, but most of them came from the maze of holes that follows the slope of the field on the south side of the Gully. Here the ferrets were busy for at least an hour and we never waited long between rabbits; sometimes there was no time to reload after a couple of shots before the next rabbit bolted. Once or twice there were two rabbits running down or across the slope at the same time. And when the failing light told us that it

was already too late to be out ferreting, that it was high time to return the ferrets to their box and take them home, by then there were sixteen rabbits for us to carry back to the Land Rover through the brown November twilight.

Rabbits in flight from the enemy are often just as testing as a climbing pheasant or a jinking woodcock. But, however difficult it might be, ferreting does lack some of the beauty and the imaginative appeal that belong to shooting things that fly; for our hearts aspire to a high pheasant or the glimpsed shape of a flighting duck; we seem, when we bring them down, to pluck them from the sky; we win them from another element and the moment of death is often very beautiful. Rabbits, by contrast, run on the ground and, when we shoot them, they stay on the ground. Shooting rabbits is an earth-bound activity; there is no lift of the spirit; there are no transfiguring glories of sky and sunlight; there are no high beauties of sudden death and graceful fall. Shooting rabbits, compared with shooting game, is shooting on a lower plane; it is humble sport for a cloudy winter afternoon, but it is often difficult and, when ferrets know their job and when rabbits respond appropriately, it is sport that should never be despised.

I drove past the hunt the other day on my way to feed my pheasants at High Park, and the sight reminded me, as it always does, that, although I do not hunt myself, I shall still feel impoverished when Mr Blair finally screws up his courage and declares an end to hunting with hounds. I shall miss stopping the Land Rover for a few minutes in the hope of spotting hounds at work on the hillside; I shall miss waving at friends as I drive past them, or pulling in to the side of the road to wind down the window and ask them how their day is going. These will, of course, be small deprivations and I shall continue to shoot and to fish; but it will be in the sad awareness that a great and kindred tradition has been shamefully done away with. And often, when I am resting by the water or waiting for the first pheasants to fly from cover, when in one way or another I am absorbing the delights of my own sports, I feel sorrow for friends who found an important part of the pleasure of their lives in an activity that always seemed wholesome to them, until at last they learned that it had always been immoral and had suddenly become illegal as well.

I shall miss my occasional encounters with the Lunesdale; I shall also feel unsettled whenever I remember that hunting has been banned; for, if it is wrong to chase foxes for the fun of it, I cannot help thinking that it must also be wrong to shoot pheasants and to kill trout for the same reason; and there is the admittedly remote danger that Mr Blair, even though he has promised that shooting and fishing are safe in Britain as long as he continues to rule it, will become briefly rational and consistent enough to recognise that, having got rid of one fieldsport, he is morally obliged to get rid of the lot of them, or at least to produce some convincing reasons for regarding hunting as an abhorrent activity while at the same time thinking of shooting and fishing as innocent pastimes. If I were a hunter, denied the practice of my sport, I should find the sight of men in waders dragging fish through the water with hooks driven into their mouths, or of men in breeches waving guns to and fro and knocking pheasants from the sky, I should find these sights bitter sights indeed; I should wonder why on earth shooters and fishers were allowed to continue with their pleasures now that mine had been declared an abomination. I should want Mr Blair to tell me what he was up to.

The trouble with fox-hunting seems to be that people enjoy it; it is the thought of men and women dressed in old-fashioned clothes and pursuing the fox for the sheer pleasure and poetry of the chase

that seems to stick in the gullets of those who want it banned. Why the enjoyment of hunting foxes is, in Mr Blair's opinion, offensive in a way that relishing the fall of a pheasant or the hooking of a trout is not, remains, however hard I try to fathom it, an impenetrable mystery to me (unless perhaps it has something to do with votes). If hunting involves the unjustifiable abuse of animals, how can fishing and shooting be acquitted of the same charge? We may eat trout and pheasants but this is an irrelevance; we go fishing and shooting for the same reason that sends our friends out hunting, which is because we enjoy catching trout and we enjoy killing pheasants; we value our enjoyment more highly than we value the lives and the comfort of pheasants and trout, and, according to Mr Blair, this relative evaluation is perfectly right and proper. What I am eager to learn is why old Charley Fox deserves special treatment. No one seems able to tell me.

I have made these or very similar points before; I shall probably make them again because they need making as often as possible. There is no special or unique cruelty about fox-hunting. Charges of animal abuse can just as convincingly be aimed at shooting and fishing and I do not see how we can sensibly grant privileges to mammals while denying them to fish and birds. The reason for banning hunting can only be the belief that it is wrong to kill animals for pleasure; if this is held to be true then fishing and shooting should go as well, and I fancy that many other pleasures should disappear along with them. If it is wrong to kill foxes I am inclined to think that it is also wrong to slaughter sheep; and before you start insisting that dead sheep serve our need to eat, whereas chasing and killing foxes is a gratuitous indulgence, let me assure you that it is not so.

Eating flesh stands in exactly the same relationship to need as does fox hunting; they are both activities that have evolved into pleasure from earlier necessity. Once, before we had learned the farmer's arts, it was necessary to hunt – not the fox, it is true, but tastier creatures – in order to put food in our bellies. Now we can chew flesh without first pursuing it through the wild wood, but we no longer need to digest animals in order to stay alive; we can live long and perfectly healthy, if not perfectly happy lives, on a diet of inanimate vegetables. We eat sheep because we enjoy the taste of it; sheep are killed in their hundreds of thousands because wine snobs like me cannot bear the thought of gurgling their claret with a mess of lentils on the plates in front of them.

What your meat-eater is declaring, with each mouthful of pork or chicken or morally abhorrent but rather delicious veal, is that he values his delight in the taste of flesh much more highly than he values the lives of those creatures to which that same flesh once belonged. I believe that he is right and I shall continue to swallow a generous quantity of (mainly red) meat on most days of the week; but even those who fret about their cholesterol levels and eat beef and lamb only on special occasions, even occasional indulgers of this sort are proclaiming, as they masticate portions of dead animal, that fox hunting, and fishing and shooting to boot, are in their opinion morally blameless activities. And there is no cruelty, there is no suffering in the field that does not find its equivalent in the abattoir, or on the way to it, or in the cages where battery chickens live out their wretched lives in order to put cheap eggs and cheap meat on supermarket shelves.

Our attitude to animals has changed over the centuries and there are those who see in this a gradual process of enlightenment: a slow progress towards ever greater respect and tenderness. Cock fighting has long been outlawed; badger and bear baiting inspire almost universal disgust, and exotic animals are no longer paraded through the streets of our cities with chains round their necks. This, the argument goes, is all part of the march of civilisation, as man grows further and further away from his rude beginnings; it is

inevitable, the argument continues, that before long this onward march will sweep away hunting, shooting and even fishing, as we learn to acknowledge that we have no right to chase or to kill animals merely because we enjoy it, or because, from the thrill of the chase and the challenge of the kill, we draw both pleasure and fulfilment.

It may be that this process really is underway, although the hidden cruelties of factory farming have turned it into a distinctly mixed blessing for many of the creatures whose lives it should have improved; this process may be unfolding and is perhaps a natural consequence of urbanisation. But I would point out here that, if indeed it is underway and if it is gathering force, then the power of its momentum must surely result in the end of meat-eating. If, however slowly, we are learning to treat animals with more respect, we must eventually stop killing them and putting bits of them into our mouths. It is a process that cannot reach its climax and fulfilment merely with the abolition of fieldsports.

This particular view of man's evolving relationship with other animals is, in my opinion, profoundly misconceived. I think that it is absurd and irreverent to renounce the sustaining pleasures of meat, absurd because it sets a false value on the worth of animals, irreverent because it refuses to acknowledge our place in nature and is at the same time a rejection of nature's best gifts. We have outlawed badger baiting and similar activities, not as the first steps of an ineluctable process that will eventually put an end to all forms of animal exploitation, but because we have come to see them as activities that demean the natural dignity of animals and at the same time brutalise men.

Now death does not demean animals. Battery cages do, but death most certainly does not. The death of a fox hunted by men is no more demeaning than the death of a rabbit hunted by a fox. It is, moreover, arguable that to kill wild animals in their prime, or at the beginning of their descent into weakness and disease and decrepitude, is an act of mercy, releasing them from the harsh fate that nature decrees for such creatures at their end. Fieldsports do not demean animals, and they do not brutalise men, for we do not fish or shoot or hunt in lust of violence or in thirst for blood, but rather to establish a contact with the life all round us, a contact that reaches way down into our own lives, expressing the depth and the complexity of our involvement with the natural world and with those other creatures that share it with us.

Through fieldsports we establish a whole and a wholesome relationship with animals: honest and unsentimental and full of admiration. Fieldsports express a vision of man as the summit of sentient creation, claiming his right to make other animals serve his pleasure and his need, but acknowledging that it should be exercised with reverence, and finding through the exercise of that same right, that he is drawn into the world of nature and embraces it with love. I know that it will sound odd and that it will puzzle, if not outrage, many of those who have no knowledge of our sports, but something of this experience lies at the heart of the devotion which every true hunter, shooter or fisherman feels for both his sport and his quarry and for the places where he finds them.

The fisherman, the shooter, the hunter, in their involvement with fish and birds and foxes, maintain that balance which is the essence of any sensible relationship with animals; they recognise the profound gulf between themselves and other creatures; they see in this their entitlement to pursue their several sports, and they make this pursuit in a spirit of praise and thanksgiving; and, though we acknowledge that our humanity sets us apart from the animals we hunt and kill, yet our sport brings us a strange and wonderful sense of communion with the rest of creation. Fieldsports are not a barbarity; they are an enrichment. They express and preserve the essential truths of the relationship between man and animals; they bind man to nature with strong ties of admiration and desire. And this is why not only I and those others like me who love the sports that belong to rivers and fields and woods, but also millions of men and women who neither hunt nor shoot nor fish will without knowing it, have been impoverished if the solemn ritual of the hunt ever becomes no more than a memory.

Chapter Six

December

*A record third shoot; what makes a challenging
pheasant; loss of form; late season grouse on
the high Pennines shooting at Wigglesworth;
views on syndicate shooting; the trophy
sportsman; pre-Christmas shoot back home*

I am embarrassed by the admission I am about to make; I shall spit
it out and get it over with, confessing that my third shoot at High
Park brought another record bag in the form of twenty-nine pheasants – I had been hoping for about twenty – plus two pigeons, one
woodcock and a rabbit. There were five guns to share the sport and
I am relieved that we shot indifferently; otherwise we might have
taken away as many as forty pheasants, which would most certainly
have been too many. I was, of course, delighted by the show of
game, but along with this delight there was just a touch of disappointment, provoked by the belief that records mean rather more
when they manage to survive a bit longer than a month; and now
there is also the danger that I shall start expecting a bag of at least
twenty pheasants from every High Park shoot, and go home
dejected whenever the day has ended with only a handful of birds to
show for it all.

I remember the time not so long ago when half a dozen birds was contentment; I remember the November afternoon five years ago when they first fell in double figures, and how I celebrated this bag of twelve birds with friends and with rabbit stew, with claret and malt whisky, with toasts to Merlin the spaniel and to all the pheasants of High Park, both the living and the dead ones; and then we raised our glasses in honour of St Hubert and of all the saints in heaven who look down with kind eyes upon the English countryside and the sports that belong there.

Undoubtedly the weather was the reason for Saturday's abundance of birds, the weather and the fact that, after lunch, we could follow the pheasants that had fled over my boundary during the morning's little drives, following them to the Gully where long experience had wrongly taught them that they would be safe. All day there was a keen wind blowing from the East and already the night had brought a thin cover of snow. Most of the time there were streaks and patches of blue in the sky and there was often sunshine in the branches; but there were also great lead-coloured clouds and, throughout the day, sleet and snow came in flurries or in brief periods of thicker fall. It was the sort of day when pheasants stay close to home, lurking deep in the gorse or beneath thick piles of brash, doing this for a change rather than choosing to exercise their indisputable and very tiresome right to roam.

I was expecting there to be birds on Beck Bank and on both sides of the wood. I was not disappointed and my guests shot some fine birds down by the sike. The warm and tangled cover on Beck Bank, the steep and sheltered sides of the wood: these are the places where you would look for pheasants on a cold and windy day in December with snow both lying on the ground and blowing on the air. What surprised me was the number of birds that flushed from the rough cover round the New Pen, for it was bleak up there with the dead rushes bending and hissing in the wind. I hoped for a bird or two and thought there might be none: there were at least a dozen of them and I was left wishing that I had stood my guns down by the sike rather than asking them to walk below the fence at intervals of twenty yards.

I was on the other side of the fence, in among the rushes with bad Digby and Merlin in my care; until bad Digby decided to go exploring by himself, slipping out through the dog-gate – he is a cunning beast – and putting on a private drive for his own amusement, flushing pheasants from the gorse in the Gutter, fast and rising birds that flew straight over the sike where there was no one to greet them. They would have been testing birds and they were all wasted and Digger was in deep disgrace. He spent the rest of the day on a lead, though even so he managed to make chaos for a time. He is a wicked dog and I have finally acknowledged that he is not fit for any form of organised shooting; he is a dog for January days when I go to High Park with no human company, seeking sport in those bits and pieces of my land that are passed over on more nearly formal occasions.

The bag at lunchtime was twelve pheasants and the woodcock and the pigeon. With a dozen pheasants already laid out on the grass, my hopes for about twenty birds seemed reasonable enough. I was well pleased as I sat beneath the hedge in the sunshine, sipping whisky and eating a pie and throwing bits of pastry over to Merlin. I thought we might get something like twenty pheasants, with perhaps another woodcock or two and a few rabbits; but I had reckoned without the Gully, which was where I took my guests as soon as our boxes and flasks were back in their bags and we were on our feet again and ready to climb Pheasant Hill.

We gave half an hour to our food and drink. As long as the weather is dry, and provided that the morning had shown some sport, I think lunch is the best part of a shooting day at High Park. I enjoy sitting on a bucket under the sky; I enjoy the presence of my

friends and the easy conversation that passes between us. I love the taste of outdoor whisky on a winter's day, whisky that is sipped with slow relish while I tell myself that there is still time for another five minutes before we move, at the same time thinking that the best of our sport may still be ahead of us.

Cloud swept in as we trudged up Pheasant Hill and then climbed the stile over the boundary fence. With the cloud came more snow, thicker that at any time during the morning, and up there on the edge of the fells the wind was strong and very cold. It was a white and a grey and a blustering world, with blurred forms and looming shapes and whirling patterns of snow. All down the long line of the Gully the dark mass of the gorse had half turned to white. The walls were white-lined and white-bottomed, with a blowing spray of snow from their notched tops; the grey trunks of the beeches merged into the paleness of the rising land, while their creaking branches flailed against the wild sky.

I placed the guns down the line of the Gully; then Austin and I went up beyond the beeches and loosed Holly and my Merlin into the gorse. The first pheasants came almost immediately, leaping into the wind and rising in seconds above the highest branches. They were wonderful, wind-charged birds; they were masters of the air, climbing steeply to heaven and curling in their climb. Some of them flung back their heads and plummeted to earth; one or two staggered as they rose and then planed flapping down. Most of them triumphed in their flight and flew on into the snow. As the dogs hunted their way down the slope, more and more birds flushed; they were now more like ordinary birds and many of them flew out on my side, away from the standing guns. They dipped and rocked in the wind but that was no excuse for my missing all but two of them.

And then suddenly there were three dogs in the gully; Holly and Merlin were meant to be there; but now there was a black and

126

white springer as well, a springer with a lead round his neck; for Digger, who had been put in the care of big Jamie, had pulled the screw of his spike clean out of the earth and was now joining madly in the fun. I caught up with him at the bottom of the Gully. He had a pheasant in his mouth and looked delighted with himself. When all was gathered in, the morning's dozen had risen to twenty-four, and such had been the chaos of Digger's contribution to the drive that many birds had risen and flown away without a shot. Perhaps, realising the imminent danger of an excessive bag, Digger had done his bit to make sure there were a few pheasants left for later days. At the time I was not hugely appreciative, although, with another twelve pheasants now added to the bag, I could not find it in my heart to hate bad Digby as bitterly as he deserved.

The Gully was the climax of the day. We finished with my own gorse; we finished in pale winter sunshine and cold, still air, for the wind died away as we climbed up from the Gully and returned to the shelter of my little valley. We shot another five birds and I ended the day with twenty-eight used cartridges in my pocket, knowing that they had only managed to shoot six pheasants (and a pigeon); but in spite of shooting badly, and in spite of the antics of the Prince of Darkness, I was very happy as I drove away from High Park into what seemed the beginning of a blizzard. And the chief part of my happiness was not the record bag lying among dogs and boots and two boys in the back of the Land Rover: it was the memory of those pheasants springing from the top of the Gully and rising into the sky with snow all round their wings, until they found the wind and rose higher still and then glided so gracefully from danger through the whirling greyness of the air. They were embodiments, those pheasants were, of all the challenge and all the beauty that binds us shooters to the sport we love.

I seem to remember, some time before the pheasant shooting began, mentioning the subject of kills to cartridges; I think I stated that I

expected to kill one head of game for roughly two and a half cartridges; I may also have mentioned that I remained more or less at ease with myself as long as the ratio did not rise much above one for three. I am an average sort of shooter and years ago it lodged in my mind from some source or other that if an average sort of shooter, involved with averagely challenging pheasants, takes an average of three cartridges to kill each of his birds, then your average sort of shooter is entitled to feel that he is doing as much as can be expected of him. You may well wonder how 'averagely challenging pheasants' are to be defined. My answer is that the term represents a range of birds, from the straightforward but still sporting, through the rather more challenging and the distinctly awkward, to the occasional pheasant of glory that, when once in a while it falls to your average shooter's swing, fills his heart with a surge of wonder and pride. It may also inspire the brief fancy that he is rather more than an average sort of shooter, a fancy that often survives no longer than the next bird, which is likely to be a very average sort of pheasant, and is likely to escape both barrels of your average but temporarily deluded shooter's gun.

Averagely challenging pheasants are found, would you believe it, on the majority of pheasant shoots, where it is general practice to leave the low and the feeble birds well alone, although there seems usually to be one among the guns who exempts himself from this commendable abstinence. The majority of pheasant shoots, at least most of those where I have stood in the line with a gun, show a pleasing variety of birds. There is not a tedious procession of pheasants flying on their way at no more than head height; neither do the drives produce a continual stream of archangels, birds forty and more yards up in the sky, birds so high that they demand special skills and special loads and lots of previous experience if the man beneath them is to have much hope of making more than an occasional contribution to the day's bag.

Average shooters, anyway, exercising what skills they possess on average pheasant shoots, should, according to my forgotten source, kill a bird with each third cartridge. I always feel pleased with myself when I manage to do better than this, and so far this season, as far as my shooting is concerned, my thoughts have been tending towards complacency. Early flights were very successful and early pheasants never inspired the feeling of hopeless incompetence that comes over most average shooters from time to time. Perhaps I was beginning to tell myself that my performance with a shotgun was just a bit above the average; perhaps I was beginning to think that I had developed into a thoroughly competent, rather than merely an average shot. Certainly I have of late been a confident shot and I dismissed my poor shooting on the most recent High Park day as nothing more than a temporary loss of form. I rather fancied that, when next I stood in a line of guns, I should find that I was doing as well, if not slightly better, than the men standing on either side of me.

The next time came within a week, for friend and fellow fives-player, John Guthrie, had invited me for a day with his pheasants at Scargill, high in the Pennines above Barnard Castle. It was a bitterly cold day. One minute the sky and the fields were full of wild sunshine; a moment later the heather hills above us were glowering beneath great masses of black cloud swept in by the wind, which also lifted pheasants from the game cover and blew flushes of them over the guns, curling and wobbling and rising as they came on.

They were high birds and they were fast birds, but they were birds well within range and they were birds of which the competent shooter should most certainly have taken his share. All round me they were stopping in the sky and falling to earth, but those that flew over my head were usually flying just as vigorously once they were behind it.

I made all sorts of excuses to myself; I had forgotten my mittens and my hands were aching with the cold and sometimes struggling with the safety catch; I had slept badly and risen early; I was feeling jaded and tired and my timing had gone to pieces; I was oppressed by all those examination scripts waiting for me to mark them when I got home; and there were all those reports to write, and the guns were too close together and I was taking too long to decide that a particular bird was mine. These were just some of the excuses that presented themselves to me for almost instant dismissal, as I stood there shivering in the wind and waiting until it was time to miss the next bird.

The grim conviction at the back of my mind had no time for such excuses; for, as each bungled bird meant that the next one had even less to fear, this same conviction kept whispering to me, raising its voice to suggest that I was missing at least five out of every six pheasants that came my way, not because I was cold or tired or preoccupied or unaccountably and temporarily off form, but because I was, quite simply, a lousy shot. The voice reminded me of other days when my shooting had been similarly incompetent; it pointed out that my good days at High Park were nothing to be proud of, since at High Park I was rarely standing where the tall pheasants came, but was up on the edges of the gorse, flushing birds for my friends and taking a few of the easy ones that flushed the wrong way.

It ended up by making me feel thoroughly ashamed of myself and profoundly dejected; and this, of course, is what shooting does to you: it persuades you that you can hit things and are a competent all-round shooting man; it fosters complacent and secretly proud illusions. Then, deciding that the time has come for humiliation, it suddenly changes your mind, making you realise that you could never shoot straight and would do much better by leaving the gun at home and concentrating on the dog.

This is more or less how I felt as I trudged back to the Land Rover at the end of the morning, knowing that I had fired almost thirty cartridges and that, between them, they had accounted for two dead pheasants and one wounded bird that had yet to be gathered. I was wondering about a stiff gin and tonic; wisely I decided on wine and, during lunch, I recovered most of my composure, resolving to forget the horrors of the morning and to shoot more efficiently in the afternoon. Shooting builds you up and then puts you down; it does this to me, at least; but I also find, as I get older, that bouts of incompetence bite somewhat less deeply than in younger days, and that the despondency they bring with them can be more easily shaken off.

These days I sometimes manage to pull myself together within the course of a day, so that, after shooting abysmally in the morning, I kill a succession of pheasants in the afternoon and go home in love with shooting again and feeling moderately pleased with myself. It does not always happen like this – and of course there are days when it happens the other way round – but, as I helped myself to another glass of John's wine and another slice of his cheese, there was steel in the soul, hardening my determination that the lead in my cartridges would be aimed more efficiently at any pheasants that flew over me during the afternoon drives.

Now John Guthrie is an adventurous spirit; he revels in snow and icy winds and stormy skies; he also thinks that they are best appreciated from the roof of England rather than half-way towards its floor. As we sat there, drinking our coffee and feeling delightfully warm, he could hear the gale rattling the windows; through them he could see the dark threat of the massing clouds. I seem to remember him saying that he had found the morning unpleasantly close; but, whether or not he passed this verdict on conditions that had chilled me to the bone, he most certainly rose from the table with a gleam in his eyes and announced that we were not, in fact, shooting pheasants in the afternoon. It was, after all, only December the seventh; a mere thousand feet above sea level was far too low and too soft for him; we were therefore heading higher, we were going up to the moor, where we should be able to breathe in the bracing air of the high Pennines and test our skills against late-season grouse.

And so it was that the Land Rover drove off for the skies, fording brown and gushing streams, sliding through deep ruts in the peat, coughing and groaning its way up steep tracks with the dark heather spreading out from them on either side. And, as the Land Rover crawled up towards the butts, so the sky turned blue and grey and black again, while great rainbows reared briefly and melted away and while ragged sheets of snow swept over the moor.

We waited in a gully for the first drive and I found, to my surprise, that I was warmer than in the morning. Remembering how some years ago, at the end of a season of plenty, I had once struggled to cope with grouse in early November, I gave myself little chance with birds a month older hurtling down a gale force wind. When at last they came they were wonderful; there were not many of them, but three or four were more than enough: dark shapes skimming the heather and bursting over me on cupped wings. They seemed like embodied spirits of the wind and the winter and the wild moorland over which they flew. They were wonderful and their sudden appearance worked something like a miracle, for three of them fell to my three shots and at last Merlin could stop shivering and spend a few minutes doing what he had come to do.

There was a genuine blizzard during the second drive; the wind raged on our backs and there was no shelter from it in a grouse butt. Suddenly my cap was plucked from my head and flung twenty yards into the heather, so that the wet flakes battered my bald patch and froze me more completely through and through. Two or three big packs crossed the line away from me, hovering on the gale and floating through the sky like black ghosts. The faint sound of gunfire seemed an insignificance in the wildness of it all. And by now I was shaking with cold and barely capable of holding a gun. I confess that I was very glad when at last I heard the dim sound of the keeper's horn, for it meant that I could stagger to the Land Rover and start the engine and turn on the heater. The inside of the Land Rover was like paradise. O yes! I was glad the drive was over and that I had found refuge from the gale; but I was much more deeply thankful that I had been up on the moor for those two afternoon drives and that, with the morning's missed pheasants a trivial recollection, I had finally witnessed the dark glory of December grouse in the wind and the snow.

On the first day of the school holidays I was up at seven o'clock (this is early for me, especially on the first day of the holidays); I was up early because I was going shooting and it is, of course, worth dragging yourself from bed on a cold morning to celebrate three weeks' freedom with a day after pheasants. I have not taken you to my syndicate shoot so far this season, which is partly because I have not been there very often myself. I have dashed down the road once or twice for the afternoon drives, but whereas an afternoon at High Park, which is less than half an hour from Sedbergh, seems almost the perfect antidote to a morning spent in a classroom, I am not sure that a thirty mile drive in an old Land Rover, nagged by the suspicion that the afternoon's shooting will have started before you get there, is quite as restful and quite as satisfactory.

There was a time when I could miss the occasional Saturday morning's teaching and spend it with a gun in my hand rather than in front of a blackboard. Unfortunately that time has passed, and the present season will probably be my last with the syndicate, which is all the more reason for me to relish the three full days that I shall spend there during the Christmas holidays. I have shot there for more than a dozen years. I am fond of the place and of the shooting it offers. It is a typical small shoot and, although this book is really about High Park, I think there is room in it for at least one day on my syndicate shoot near Settle.

It is on the edge of a little village called Wigglesworth, which is undoubtedly a ridiculous name, perhaps even more ridiculous than Giggleswick a few miles away. In spite of its name, Wigglesworth is a pretty spot and I was very happy to be driving towards it on the first day of the holidays. It was also a very pretty day, with frosty fields and a blue sky, with the heater full on and with the low sun shining horizontally onto all the dust and grease that had gathered on the inside of my windscreen. There were times when steering the Land Rover was largely a matter of guesswork;

but Merlin and I both made it to Wigglesworth through the dazzling radiance; by nine o'clock we had drawn up in the car-park of a pub called The Plough, and shortly after I was busy smoking and drinking tea and talking to the keeper about pheasants. Some of the other guns had already turned up and I talked to them as well, though not exclusively about pheasants.

I always enjoy this prelude to a shooting day, especially if the sun is shining on the first day of the Christmas holidays, and if the air is sharp and your fingers are mittened against the cold and you stamp your feet on the earth – or the tarmac – to encourage them to start feeling warm. More guns and more beaters turn up. Dogs cavort round the vehicles or sit obediently next to their masters (Merlin stays in the Land Rover until we are ready to start); the sequence of drives will probably be explained; it may be decided to surround the duck pond and see what gets off. Whatever is decided the draw is made at last; the guns immediately work out where this will put them for the best drives, and then a cavalcade of Land Rovers and Range Rovers, together with imported variations on the same theme, moves off for the beginning of the shooting.

On Saturday we started with a little planting called Bradley Moor. It is on the edge of the shoot; it is tangled and overgrown and, although it is sometimes favoured by woodcock, there are not often many pheasants there. As number six I did not expect much to come my way, and both my barrels were wide of the one bird that did. It was not a testing bird and it should have been shot; but it takes more than a single failure to unsettle me: it is when two or three birds have flown on in spite of my attempts to stop them that I begin to dread the beginning of a day of shame. After my recent performance at Scargill I admit that even one bungled opportunity inspired a few misgivings, but then I killed the next two birds that came over me and this brought us to lunch, bringing me back to The Plough in a mood of very quiet contentment. Not many birds had been shot, but the three drives had been minor ones, with all the best shooting kept back for the afternoon. I am perfectly happy with little drives, even with lousy pegs at them, as long as the sun is shining and the frost has gone from the fields and I can hit a bird or two to give old Merlin the bliss of a retrieve.

In The Plough you can eat your lunch in the tap-room or the lounge-bar. As you would expect, the guns gather in the posh end, but they gather there without me. I prefer tap-rooms to lounge bars, preferring as a rule the company to be found in them. During shooting lunches, moreover, the guns tend to talk about stocks and shares and triumphs of speculation and the prospects for good business in the coming year, whereas beaters and keepers talk about dogs and sport. This seems to me a good reason for sitting on a hard bench in the tap-room and joining in the shooting talk, at the same time eating sausage and chips and drinking two small bottles of Guinness.

On Saturday I talked mainly with Phil the keeper. He is a good friend and he is coming to High Park for my fiftieth birthday shoot in a few days time. For the great occasion I predicted a bag of between a dozen and twenty birds (perhaps I am becoming over-confident); then we began to grumble about one or two of the Wigglesworth guns who cannot resist, or do not even try to resist, shooting low birds; then we talked about dogs for a while before moving on to the prospects for the afternoon. It was not polished or profound conversation, but it kept me very happy for three quarters of an hour until it was time to get up from the bench and go shooting again.

The main woods at Wigglesworth line the steep banks that rise from a stream unromantically but expressively called Stinking Beck. It runs over some deposits of sulphur, if that is a geographical possibility in North Yorkshire. It runs over something, anyway, and

there are days when the air is full of the stench of decay. On Saturday Stinking Beck was in one of its genial moods and the air above and all round it was pure. I was at number four peg for the first drive, which is possibly the best place to be, standing at the bottom of the slope with a covert rising up to my left. The main release pen is in the firs at the top of the wood and the drive is taken up to the pen; the beck is flowing towards and past me on my right and the trees that run steeply down to its far bank extend forty or fifty yards behind me.

There are guns over the beck, standing in little clearings and, though I cannot see them, I know that they will be peering up expectantly through the branches in the hope of fleeting chances at high and gliding and slanting shapes of pheasants. These guns are all in front of me on the right; there is another gun up the slope on my left and another beyond him. We are there for pheasants that break out from the side of the drive and all three of us know that most of these birds will come over me, high but not usually very high, fast but not usually with set wings: good sporting birds of which a gun in fair form should take a fair toll. There is time to see them, but they do not come on towards you from a swing-inhibiting distance: you see them; you lift on to them smoothly and, if you know what you are doing, there is no reason why they should not fall. Number four peg is a good place to be, standing there with your gun, listening to the tapping of the beaters' sticks and the first shouts of 'over' as the first pheasants rise and fly straight down the line of the slope, passing over the guns waiting on the other side of the beck.

On Saturday I watched these early birds with delight, for they were shining as they flew; some flapped their wings, some glided and some curled; some rose in their flight and soared way above the treetops; others swooped down the line of the slope and seemed almost to dive into the firs beyond the beck. Perhaps half a dozen crumpled and fell. My turn came in the later stages of the drive and honesty compels me to admit that I shot well. There were four pheasants and a woodcock for Merlin to gather when the horn had blown and it was time for my old spaniel to enjoy himself. While Merlin picked up my birds, I picked up eight spent cartridges and felt quietly pleased with myself.

There were three more drives. I missed two pheasants; killed two more and another woodcock and went home contented. I had shot more than adequately (ten birds for nineteen cartridges); the sun had shone all day and given fine views of the Yorkshire hills; the birds had flown well and, though the morning drives had been thin, those in the afternoon had sent plenty of pheasants over the guns, with a day's bag of 41 and 2 woodcock. Both the woodcock, moreover, were coming home with me in the Land Rover, which meant there was a little feast to look forward to some time before long. There was the thought of three weeks' holiday stretching in front of me; there was my birthday shoot at High Park in just three days; the prospect from my Land Rover, as I drove home from Wigglesworth with the sun behind me and a clear view through the windscreen, was altogether very cheering.

I thought about syndicate shooting as I drove on my way through the evening glow. I had enjoyed the day; in particular I had relished the fact that it had been a full day rather than merely an afternoon snatched from school. I had enjoyed shooting competently and I had, for the most part, enjoyed watching other people shoot. I had enjoyed most of the company and my lunch in the tap-room of The Plough had been very enjoyable indeed.

But there are drawbacks to syndicate shooting and one of them is the other guns. There are, of course, syndicates consisting of groups of close friends, who may have grown up together and have certainly shot together for many years. There is no problem here.

There are syndicates, and these are probably the best sort, where a shoot-owner invites half a dozen men he likes to share his shooting and to share the cost of it all. But there are other syndicates, and Wigglesworth is one of them, where the team of guns is not held together by ties of long familiarity or affection. We are a team that meets to shoot and that, more or less, is the beginning and end of our association. We seem to get on with each other well enough, though there are differences of interpretation about how high a driven pheasant should be before a shooter raises his gun to have a shot at it. We rub along together pleasantly enough, even though one or two of us are prone to edge in towards the coverts to get in range of undemanding birds. Wigglesworth days pass in fair good humour among the guns; but, if I were forming my own syndicate, I do not suppose that I should choose any of them as a member of my team; and I am quite certain that, if one of them were doing the same, my name would only appear on his list after he had tried twenty or thirty names and found that he was still short of a gun.

The members of my syndicate are held together by financial convenience; that is the only bond and I fancy it is not infrequently so. Shooting is undoubtedly more enjoyable among real friends, which is, of course, one of the reasons I so love my High Park days. I have another more important reservation about syndicate shooting, or rather about driven shooting in general, which is that it is far too easy. This statement will come as a particular shock to any of you who have shot driven birds in my company; if you belong to that privileged band you cannot have failed to notice how many of them I miss.

But in saying that driven shooting is too easy I am not, in fact, thinking of the pheasants that fly over me and so frequently fly on. I am thinking rather of the demands, other than the challenge of hitting well shown birds, that driven shooting makes on the men who take part in it, not the demands of skill with a gun, but the demands of knowledge and fitness and patience and understanding; I am thinking of these demands and also of the willingness to be satisfied with small rewards. For the truth is that driven shooting demands no knowledge of the ways of game from the man standing at a peg and waiting for the first pheasant to come over him; the need for this knowledge has been delegated to the keeper. It calls for little or no energy or endurance, since it is the beaters and the dogs who do all the hard work. And driven shooting rarely asks a shooting man to go home at the end of the day, thinking that he has let off his gun only once but that he has nevertheless enjoyed himself enormously.

In these respects driven shooting is an undemanding sport and because of this it often appeals to men whose interest in shooting and the countryside is superficial. Such men like a change of air at the weekends; they may well think that in buying a Range Rover and proclaiming themselves shooting men they have somehow enhanced their social status. Whether or not this is the case, they have discovered the strange satisfaction to be found in pulling a trigger and connecting with a moving target. They have probably learned this through a few lessons at a shooting school; they have enough money in the bank to pay for their shooting days. They have got themselves a pair of breeches and a sweater adorned with images of pheasants. They may also wear a tie that bears witness to their new enthusiasm; with or without such a tie they are ready to climb into the four-by-four and to head off for the country in order to start reducing its store of feathered game.

There is nothing much wrong with any of this as long as it is just a beginning: a beginning from which the novice gun goes on to absorb and to appreciate the graceful traditions of his sport and to learn something at least of all that goes into the making of a successful driven day, which should also begin to produce for him a wealth of pleasures apart from the central pleasure of his shooting:

pleasure in the performance of other guns, pleasure in the contribution of dogs and beaters and pickers-up, pleasure in the skillful management of a difficult drive, pleasure in surroundings that are often very beautiful and have often been partially shaped by the sport in which he is participating, pleasure in all the life that belongs there, not just in the winged life which he is there to harvest with his gun.

It is good that men without the knowledge or strength or time or inclination to make their sport for themselves can pay others to do it for them and learn about shooting by standing at a peg; it means that those without much experience of the countryside can begin to appreciate some of the richness of its sporting traditions. It is good that the pleasures of driven shooting are no longer reserved for those of inordinate wealth or privileged birth. It is natural that a man new to driven shooting should initially be preoccupied with his own small part in the proceedings; but it is all wrong if he remains so, if he remains self-absorbed and immature, if he does not learn to admire the birds that he shoots, if he cannot learn to respect the men who join him for the shooting and those other men who make the shooting possible; if, in short, his driven days do not bring with them a generous and thankful appreciation of all that goes into the making of them, and of all those incidental but deep delights that help to make a good driven day a rewarding and beautiful experience. If he cannot develop along these lines, then your convert to driven shooting should, in my opinion, sell his gun and watch television in his spare time, or he should take up golf and bore his friends rigid with endless descriptions of his latest round, or he could spend his Saturday afternoons making loud noises at football matches, because he will never, even if he turns into a killing shot, develop into a proper shooter.

Most of the men you meet at a driven shoot are interested in every aspect of their sport; most of them are a pleasure to stand next

December

And there was much to give pleasure and much that deserved praise on my birthday shoot. There was the taste of sloe gin (just a drop or two) in the middle of the morning; there was the taste of Glenmorangie (only a very small dram) at lunchtime; there was the feel of the hard earth under our boots, and the cunning of the pheasants that slipped away from Beck Bank when I thought that I had them surrounded. There were the shapes of bare trees against the grey sky; there was the polished gleam of the green hollies and the red glow of their clustered berries, with the dark water and the white foam of the sike rushing below them. There were pheasants that did not sneak away before the dogs could flush them over the guns; they were fast birds and they climbed steeply from Beck Bank, from the Strips and the Whins and the Gutter and from the Gully and from all my little drives. There were woodcock as well as pheasants, although most of them flushed away from danger, but two of them were shot and one of them was mine, reminding me that I now had enough of them for a solitary woodcock feast with half a bottle of burgundy. Old Merlin forgot all about his stiff joints and worked like a Trojan. And I found the thought of being fifty easy to bear, telling myself that, even in another thirty years, I might still be above ground, still able to lift a gun to my shoulder and bring an occasional pheasant crashing down to earth.

The bag for my birthday shoot was a delight to me. It was not, thank God, another record, but with the last shot fired and the last bird gathered, we laid seventeen pheasants in line beneath the hedge by the meadow gate, and beside them were two rabbits and the couple of woodcock already mentioned. In the end, too, I was pleased with my own contribution to the bag, although things went badly for most of the day, raising the fear that, after recent incompetence at Scargill and, in spite of a better performance at my syndicate shoot near Settle, I was about to enter one of those dismal periods of my shooting life when killing pheasants with any degree of consistency turns into an impossible dream.

I did not shoot well on my fiftieth birthday shoot. By three o'clock I had killed just two birds, and one of these was a jackdaw that had flapped very slowly away from one of the hoppers on the Rise, filling me with briefly efficient anger when I thought of all that plundered grain. There was this corn-heavy jackdaw and there was a hen pheasant; and the knowledge that it had taken me nine cartridges to kill them was provoking some sense of despondency. But then, right at the end of the day, there was a sudden rush of birds from the deepest tangles of the Whins. Most of them came over me and, glory be, four of them, including the woodcock, fell to my four shots, convincing me in the course of a few minutes that I was a mighty shooter of game, perhaps not just as lethal as, say, Lord Walsingham in his prime, but most definitely in the same league.

It is good when your form returns, especially when you are beginning to wonder whether old age is catching up with you and whether it has deserted you for good; it is good to feel that there is once again some point in carrying a gun and raising it to your shoulder now and then. And when this happens on your fiftieth birthday, with claret and company waiting for you in the evening, then, once the shooting is over, you walk down the fields in deep contentment, thankful for the day's sport and already looking forward to the pleasures of the evening. But you do not rush to be gone and to be splashing around in the bath.

There will be half a mug of tea still in your flask and you will drink this when you have rubbed down the dogs and stowed your gun and taken off your muddy boots. You will drink and talk and, if you are me, you will smoke for a time, while the light begins to deepen and pheasants begin to shout before going up to roost. You will talk about birds and dogs and other men's shoots; you will go over some of the day's more notable incidents; you will discuss shooting days that lie ahead, hoping for hard weather and a keen wind and for high birds. And the time will come to shake hands and

to wish well and to drive away; and, if it is your fiftieth birthday and you are due at a friend's table at eight o'clock, then as your Land Rover rumbles through the falling darkness and the shapes of the surrounding fells disappear into the night, you will feel what a blessing it is to be alive and you will hope that it continues for at least a few more years.

CHAPTER SEVEN

JANUARY

Mr Killjoy; my New Year shoot; spontaneous
sport; a perfect driven day; Digby delights
me; the going-away pheasant; flighting a
frozen pond; great moments in a shooting life

I spent Christmas with my brother and his wife in Harrow. There
was no Boxing Day shoot for me this year. I saw no hounds drawing
any of the local parks with pink-coated riders in attendance. I never
once heard the sound of a huntsman's horn or the report of a
shotgun. In spite of this I enjoyed my suburban Christmas, but after
three or four days of it I was homesick for my hills; I was also
impatient to get out to High Park and to refill the hoppers and to see
that all was well. Mr Blair did not invite me to greet the dawn of a
new millennium under the shelter of his brand new dome; and since,
to my knowledge, Mr Blair's dome contains no Fieldsports Zone, I
confess that my omission from the guest-list came as something of
a relief; it meant that I was able to get home and feed my birds and
potter round happily making ready for my next shoot on New Year's
Day.

It also meant that I could observe my long-established tradition of going to bed before midnight on New Year's Eve. You can call me Mr Killjoy, if you will, but it is only this one evening of the year that transforms me into a misanthropic recluse. Usually I am a convivial sort of fellow, but on New Year's Eve the thought of all that forced jollity and dutiful self-indulgence turns my stomach, while the prospect of singing Auld Lang Syne – what on earth does it mean, by the way? – the prospect of joining hands at midnight and drunkenly wailing a verse of Scotch gibberish fills me with loathing and dread. This year, of course, there was the further consideration that, having reached fifty, I now need to take special care of myself; and another motive for going up to roost early was my admirable ambition to shoot the first pheasant of Christendom's new millennium.

On my way to High Park the next morning there seemed hope that this ambition might be realised, for the road was very obviously uncongested by sportsmen's vehicles taking their owners to the coverts. I guessed that most shooters were still in bed and not planning to rise much before ten o'clock; I also fancied that, when at last they decided to face the day on two legs, very few of them would welcome the repeated bark of gunfire as the best tonic for dyspepsia and a sore head. I confess that, as the Land Rover chugged along almost empty roads on its way to Brough, I was thinking of myself as the model of restraint. I decided that a generous glass of dry sherry – I cannot do with those pygmy glasses into which sherry is so often poured – followed by half a bottle of red wine and a single dollop of Glenmorangie before bed, I decided that this was what the prudent shooter drinks in the evening if he wants to feel healthy and vigorous for his sport the next morning.

There were five of us at High Park for the first shoot of a new era, all very clearly undemoralised by excess. Two of my companions, in fact, claimed to have been in bed before their host, and so there was no need for us to drag ourselves unwillingly up the valley.

We almost pranced over the meadow, and our dogs were soon hunting through the gorse and the brambles. There had been ice on the edge of the roads as I drove out to High Park; but once the sun climbed a little higher the air turned as soft as May. It was hardly ideal weather for finding January pheasants at home, and we saw few birds in the morning, but it was impossible not to welcome the warmth of the sun and the shine of it on the climbing banks and in all the branches. And, although pheasants were difficult to find before noon, I reminded myself that, throughout November and December, High Park had been very kind to me, so that it would be unfair and ungrateful of me to brood resentfully if it found that it could no longer be quite so generous now that January had come along.

I doubt if I, or any of my friends, shot the first pheasant of the new century and the new millennium. I missed the first two that came my way, though I made up for this in the afternoon. At lunchtime, as we sat in the sunshine under the hedge, there was only one bird in the bag, and that had been shot well after noon. Doubtless most shooters, having risen late this first of January, left their guns in their cupboards for the rest of the day, but I am sure, now I think about it, that some hardy sportsman was out at dawn and had bagged his first bird while I was still on my way to Brough. I offer him my heartiest congratulations.

In the afternoon the bag rose quickly. A breeze sprang up and the birds curled on it as they crossed the guns; they rose from those two little patches of gorse on the ridge of the high pasture above the Gully; they rose from the Gully itself; from the rushy field in which the Gully begins and, back on my land, they flushed from the thick spread of gorse on North Bank. I had missed the two birds the morning offered me, but I took all my five chances in the afternoon. A pattern seems to be emerging to my form at the moment: a pattern of early incompetence followed by a sudden improvement after lunch. It is by no means an ideal pattern but it is most certainly a lot better than the reverse.

We finished the day with seventeen dead pheasants: the same number as last time, though on this occasion there were no woodcock or rabbits to add variety to the bag. At the end of my millennium shoot I suddenly realised that High Park had for the first time given me more than a hundred pheasants in a season, which is a fine achievement for a shoot that puts down only one hundred and fifty birds and extends over little more than a hundred acres. I also realised that there was still a month of the season to go, and I wondered how many more pheasants those four weeks might add to the columns of my game book. I felt very proud of High Park, but not just – or chiefly – for the wealth of pheasants it has produced this winter. I acknowledged with deep gratitude that my friends and I had enjoyed five days full of beauty and interest and excitement, not to mention three duck flights and a delightful outside afternoon. Those hundred pheasants meant a lot to me, but the days would still have been great days if, between them, they had only produced, say, ninety birds.

I drove home that evening full of contentment, looking forward to the second half of my New Year's Eve burgundy (not preceded by sherry but most definitely to be followed by a splash or two of Glenmorangie); but it was not only wine and whisky that I was looking forward to. There was also the less immediate prospect of back-end days among my pheasants, days when pheasants fly with a challenge and a defiance that stirs the hearts of those who would bring them down to earth, days on which the pleasure of our sport is sharpened by the approach of the season's end, impromptu days that can even find room for bad Digby running wild in the depths of the gorse. I thought of these pleasures now lying ahead of me and, in particular, I thought of a long sloping field on my rented ground, a field where we have yet to go. It is covered from top to bottom

with rushes and brambles and gorse. I have often watched birds flying there from the Gully, and determined to bide my time. I have been saving it for January and the time has now come. The pheasants that seek refuge in the rough field across the road are in for a little surprise.

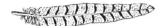

In January I shoot at High Park almost as often as I choose. New Year's Day brings the last of the five shoots for which invitations are issued whole weeks in advance. January is the month when I shoot on impulse, because the sun is shining or because the wind is blowing from the right direction or because it is raining and I want to go shooting in spite of the rain. One of the delights of having your own ground is that, in January, you can wake up in the morning and decide immediately, or perhaps while shaving, or even over breakfast, or conceivably as late as eleven o'clock; you can decide at almost any time before noon that you are going to spend a few hours out with a gun and a dog, exploring some of those nooks and corners of your shoot that have so far been overlooked.

Earlier in the season I resist this sort of temptation; earlier in the season I am thinking of those five great days. But come the second of January and those five days, whether or not they turned out to be as great as I was hoping, are now behind me. Come the second of January, and I can surrender to temptation without a prick of guilt; while, by the middle of January, the lengthening evening light means that, even if you only start after lunch, you will still have plenty of time to wander here and there in search of a shot or two.

Sometimes it will be just you and your dog, or you may ring a friend and ask him to join you; if you are a schoolmaster you may take along a couple of boys to carry the game bags and help to fill

them. Whether you are alone or in company your expectations will be easy, and you will find this one of the great delights of your January days: three or four pheasants, with perhaps a few rabbits, will be more than enough to send you home a happy man. Even a single shot and a single bird may do the trick. There have even been January days when I have roamed High Park without ever lifting my gun to my shoulder and have still managed to go home feeling glad to have been out there.

Before there came a chance for a January day at High Park, there was some sport of a very different sort. Early in the year I was a guest at a driven shoot in North Yorkshire. We shot 184 pheasants, one woodcock and one jay. The birds flew well and I shot well and enjoyed myself rather less than you might have expected. To begin with there were mutterings among the guns about slack beating, thought to be a deliberate ploy designed to ensure plenty of birds for the beaters' shoot at the end of the month. I could not understand these mutterings, since every drive sent a continual stream of pheasants over the line; they seemed mean-spirited and selfish mutterings to me and they ate into my pleasure. There were these mutterings and there was also a pervading and very tedious coarseness to the conversation that filled in the intervals between drives. And the guns, at the end of it all, were eager to kill more birds, as though 184 pheasants had not been enough for them. It took stern words from the shoot captain to persuade them that the day's shooting was over and that some birds must be kept for the rest of their January sport. The meal after the shoot was full of obscene and humourless jokes; it was also full of wine, beer and whisky and it was very clearly going to last for a long time. I toyed with a glass of wine, laughed at the obscenities in a cowardly fashion, made my excuses as soon as possible, and drove off into the night.

The journey home took me about two hours and I spent some of it, after my experience of a seriously flawed day's driven shooting, constructing my perfect day of the same sort: a day with no mutterings or complaints from the guns, a day without cheap and tedious humour, but most certainly not a day without booze. I made good progress with my perfect driven day on the way home, until my mind wandered off in other directions and left it somewhere just before lunch. From time to time over the last few days I have returned to it and moved things on, so that now it is more or less complete.

In describing my perfect driven day to you I shall start at the wrong end of it by considering first of all the perfect bag. I am well aware that every shooter, if asked his opinion on this subject, will come up with a different answer. Just a few men think that as many as possible is always best. The guns on the North Yorkshire shoot were most certainly of this persuasion, but most of us, I fancy, believe that a day can bring too many birds. The biggest day in which I ever took part finished with 250 of them; they were very demanding birds and I relished making my modest contribution to so huge a total; but I do not want an enormous number of dead birds at the end of my perfect driven day: it seems to me that we can pull our triggers too often, and it is good, when looking back on a day's sport, to be able to remember every bird that fell to your gun. My perfect driven day would not see the death of 200 pheasants; it would put more birds in the sky than I am used to seeing, and it would bring just over a hundred of them falling to the earth.

It will take place in early January, when birds are strong on the wing and flush less predictably. The pheasants, of course, will be fast and they will fly at a good height, but I do not want them all at the limit of range because, in that case, I shall hit very few of them and go home feeling miserable. Good, fast, hittable birds are what I want for my perfect day, with just a few of them heading for heaven and so offering the chance of a really memorable shot.

Pheasants fly best with a wind to help them on their way, and so my perfect day will have a stiff breeze blowing through it, with pale sunshine between broken cloud and no fear of rain. There will be frost on the fields, but the air will soften in the sun and by noon the ground, except under the trees and in the shadow of steep banks, will be yielding to my boot. I like a frost that grips and refuses to let go, but such weather is for rough shooting; it is weather for following an eager spaniel along the hedges rather than for shivering on the edge of a covert. My perfect day will be a day of little drives, nine or ten of them, and each drive will offer most of the eight guns three or four chances. We shall walk between stands and we shall be walking through a northern valley and through familiar countryside. Once or twice I shall find myself standing on the edge of a river that I fish during the trout season, so that, while waiting for the pheasants, I can light my pipe and think of trouting. In this way I shall see my shooting landscape in a deeper and a richer context, and I shall love it more.

Most of my fellow guns will already be friends, though it is always good to meet someone you do not know and to discover that your shooting thoughts are broadly similar. I shall be the only schoolmaster in the party, which will make tedious talk about education less likely to interfere with my pleasure. None of the guns, by the way, will have a beard. There will be ten minutes for comforts half-way through the morning, which will consist of damson or sloe gin rather than buckshot. We shall eat in the middle of the day, for, although on short winter days I appreciate the reason for shooting straight through, I prefer my lunch when there is still the prospect of more sport to follow. Let it be a simple meal, let it be a pie and a sandwich eaten in a barn with a generous dram to chase away the cold (I have, incidentally, just poured myself one). Whatever form lunch takes, it should not last much longer than three quarters of an hour.

You will not be surprised to learn that my perfect driven day will find me on form, though I may shoot badly on the first drive and be doubly delighted thereafter to realise that I have rediscovered the knack of hitting pheasants. But, even if I shoot well throughout the day, a bird here and there will catch me unprepared, or be just too high or too fast for me since, in order to enjoy killing birds, I need to experience the disappointment of missing just a few of them. I shall shoot fifteen or sixteen pheasants on my perfect day, firing something like twenty five cartridges. My last bird of the day will also be my best bird of the day; it will be a long way up in the sky, where it will throw back its head and then descend to the earth like a feathered stone.

I am enjoying my perfect day so much that I am feeling tempted to pour myself another whisky and prolong the pleasure by adding on another drive or two, or perhaps an evening flight. On my perfect day, anyway, I shall have a dog sitting at my peg and it will not be Digby. Old Merlin will be there with me and, though most of the birds I shoot will be dead before they hit the ground, there will be a runner or two, so that Merlin can make light of his stiff joints, hunting my runners down and bringing them in to me.

I have forgotten woodcock, but there will certainly be a few of them. I shall be happy with just one to my gun, although I should be delighted to be given a couple to take home. At the end of the day we shall all declare that things could not have gone better; we shall stand round talking to the beaters about the day's drives and how well they managed them; we shall praise the keeper for the quality of the birds and for his expertise in showing them at their best. Deciding that it is time to go we shall slip him an appropriate tip; but then, unwilling to admit that it is all over, we shall linger by the vehicles and talk about shooting a little longer. One by one we shall drive off and, when at last I climb into the Land Rover, home will be no more than an hour away.

During the journey I shall realise that at last I have experienced the perfect driven day and that perfection demands my best claret. I shall ask myself whether there is still a bottle of Pichon Lalande '83 in my cellar and, when I get home, I shall discover that there is. I shall decant half of it into a half-bottle and cork it up, leaving the other half to settle and breathe while I lie in the bath and then faff around and write up the game book and then bring out the fillet steak. And the ending of this perfect day will itself be perfect if I can tell myself, while drinking a glass of Glenmorangie before going to bed, that tomorrow is another shooting day: not a driven day this time, but a day for bad Digby, a rough day along hedges and ditches, among rushes and brambles in search of snipe and woodcock and rabbits and the odd pheasant. And perhaps this day, too, will in its own way come close to perfection. And if it does excel itself and turn into a red-letter day of the rough-shooting sort, then there will be the second half of the Pichon Lalande waiting to honour it in the evening. I shall, of course, drink it whatever happens.

Just before the end of the Christmas holidays, after spending the morning fiddling round with words, I suddenly felt weary of writing and knew at once that it was time to go in search of a January pheasant or two. We were out at High Park in less than an hour, just Digby and I, with the wet fields and the pale sunshine all round us, with pools of water in every hollow and with a squelch at every step. I was tempted to head straight for my rented ground and for the field that has yet to be investigated, the field that, with its rushes and its gorse and bramble thickets, seemed sure to be hiding pheasants and rabbits for a wild spaniel to flush. I almost set off there, but then it occurred to me that this field and its secrets might be better explored with a friend or two in attendance. I had a feeling that this field was likely to be full of excitements; I thought that it would be selfish for me to enjoy them all by myself, and I also thought that I might fail to do them full justice with no gun but my own.

Putting the temptations of virgin ground sternly behind me, I set of for the Stackhole and to a dense bed of rushes below the spring that rises near the fence on its eastern edge. Digby plunged in and almost at once a cock pheasant sprang into the sunshine, throwing up a shining spray of water when he promptly fell down. He was an old bird with long spurs, a bird for the casserole rather than the roasting tray; his tail was well over two feet long and, even when splattered with mud, the sheen on his feathers was a marvel of beauty. He was a fine beginning to a January afternoon with the gun and, only minutes later, a hen joined him in the game bag; she rose from the bottom corner of the field. Digby had pushed rather too far ahead and I was pleased with the long crossing shot that brought her down. I was pleased with Digby too, in spite of his ill-disciplined eagerness; for he now chose to remind me that, when he feels in the mood, he can retrieve pheasants like a field trial champion, with his head held high and his bird held softly until delivered on command into his master's hand. He does not often feel in the mood, but it visits him now and then, and it is some time now – a year or two in fact – since he settled down to eat a pheasant in the field, deaf to all my bellowings while my friends tried politely to look the other way and almost managed not to smile.

My sport did not continue quite as it had begun; there was not a bird in every patch of rushes or in every clump of gorse. The rabbits in the Hag flushed out of shot and there were no pheasants at all; there were none in the straggling gorse bushes along my Northern boundary; but the sun was bright and the wet earth shone and it was good to feel the weight of that hen and that old cock in the game bag. It was good to stop and smoke for a while before sliding down to the sike and struggling up the muddy bank on the other side; and there, up in those patches of gorse above the Gully, up there in the sunshine Digger found two more pheasants and I shot them both and immediately decided that four pheasants were enough for the afternoon. It had lasted less than two hours, but every

minute of it had been full of expectation, except I suppose for those minutes spent sitting and smoking, which had been minutes full of quiet thoughts and of easy contentment. They are an essential part, those restful minutes and the thoughts that belong to them, of any solitary shooting day, even of a shooting day that lasts for no more than two hours. The bag, anyway, was heavy as I trudged down the fields through the pale slant of the winter sun, so heavy that I took out that long-spurred cock and admired him all over again and then carried him by hand. The duck pond needed a bucketful of grain from the back of the Land Rover; the feathers on the edge of the water told me that it would soon be time for another flight. Then it was back to Sedbergh and another tussle with words, until seven o'clock put me in the bath in preparation for putting myself an hour later at the table of a friend.

It was about ten days before I gave into temptation again. Term had started and so, although it was Saturday, I could not get away from school until half past eleven. Two boys and bad Digby were the partners of my escape. Digby was at work shortly after noon and, for the next three hours, he gave us the sort of sport that is, in my opinion, the best sport of all. There were rabbits, there were pheasants, there were snipe and woodcock; there was the excitement of shooting the field over the road for the first time, and of finding that it was very close to a rough shooter's heaven: not only full of gorse and brambles, but with boggy beds of rushes everywhere in between, and with a boggier, a more oozy and splashy hollow, a sort of wide ditch, running more or less down its middle, a hollow so splashy and so oozy that here and there it turned into running water. It was from this hollow that the snipe, a wisp of seven or eight, sprang into the air and took us by surprise. From the gorse on the sides of the hollow at least half a dozen woodcock flushed. There were rabbits in the rushes; three or four pheasants clattered onto the wing. There was the hope of a shot wherever we went among the rushes and the gorse and the oozes and the

splashes; for a few minutes there was a soft fall of snow with white flakes shining in the sunshine. I should have stood the boys at the bottom of the field and worked Digby down towards them. There would have been more shooting and less watching. But we left the Far Pasture, which is what it is now called, with a snipe and a rabbit and a woodcock and three pheasants to show for Digby's efforts there.

All through the afternoon Digby worked tirelessly, while cloud came in and then cleared again to cold sunshine. He found plenty of pheasants, though often, with the low cunning of late-season birds, they flushed away from our guns; but sometimes they flew over one of us and sometimes they came down. We finished the day with six of them, and with two woodcock and two rabbits and just the one snipe. But that snipe was the first young Jamie had ever shot and so, for one of us at least, it was a red-letter day.

It was a special day for me as well, for it gave me the sort of shooting that I most love, and there was also the pleasure of exploring a new place for the first time. On top of all this Digby behaved himself as never before. Doubtless a serious dog-handler would still have insisted that he should be retired on the spot, but my standards are less exacting than those of serious dog-handlers. I was delighted with Digby and declared to him that I should never again stick rude words in front of his name, or denounce him in company as the Beast of Brough, not even if he resumed his former habit of eating pheasants rather than bringing them somewhere near his master; for on this day of his glory he plunged into cover whenever asked, which is, in fact unremarkable because it is something that he has always done; but he also – and this is the miracle – he also came out of it more or less promptly whenever my whistle suggested to him that he should. He searched for dead and wounded game and, when he found it, he neither bit nor chewed it, but brought it almost to my hand. He worked as only a spaniel can and, when it was all

over, he stood there by the meadow gate, caked with mud and steaming and looking as only spaniels do at the end of a shooting day. I suppose I should like to have a perfect gundog – it would be good to approach a day's rough shooting without wondering whether Digby was going to ruin it all – but there are consolations to shooting over a spaniel that falls very far short of perfection. Perhaps the best of them come on those rare occasions when he chooses to imitate his betters, deciding, just for a change, to do nearly everything that he is told to do.

Digby, at any rate, was a delight to me, as was the sight of so many woodcock (we must have flushed at least a dozen). The weather was a delight to me, with the cold air and the brief flurries of snow and the alternation of bright and grey light throughout the afternoon. My young companions were a delight to me, with their polite ways and their passionate eagerness for sport. And January pheasants are almost always a delight to me; they are so strong on the wing and you must go looking for them in wild and tangled places where you never thought to look in November and December when pheasants were easy to find. It was very nearly a perfect shooting day, except that I had left my tobacco in Sedbergh and could only chew the end of an empty pipe whenever the longing came over me. There was little comfort in it and I selfishly refused to stay and flight Low Park Pond; I was so desperate to get home and fill my lungs with smoke.

Three ungathered pheasants were an even more serious blemish, all three of them hard-hit birds that tumbled from the sky and then frustrated Digby's inefficient efforts to find them, so that in the end they had to be left for the foxes. The truth is, of course, that Digby, even on his best days, is unmethodical in the way he searches for shot game. He charges round and follows three or four different scent-lines at the same time; if he smells a rabbit he forgets that he is looking for a pheasant; if he flushes a pheasant he forgets that he is in search of a dead or wounded bird. He lacks steady purpose and he fails with birds that old Merlin would find four times out of five.

Those three ungathered birds were a more serious blemish on the day than my forgotten tobacco pouch, especially since I had been preening myself with the thought that, this season at High Park, barely a single wounded pheasant had defeated the noses of our dogs. Those three birds cast a shadow over my memories of the day, but they were still rich and happy memories and, as I drank my claret the same evening and wondered about a glass of port, I knew that, with the season's end now less than three weeks away, it would not be long before the old urge seized me again, sending me off to Brough in the hope that this time perfection might just be achieved.

Now and then I hear it said, usually by men fortunate enough to spend most of their pheasant days knocking driven birds from the sky, that the going-away pheasant is an altogether unworthy target for their guns and that, even though it is too easy to be worth bothering with, it is also far too often wounded rather than killed. Pheasants, according to these sporting connoisseurs, should be shot in the head or not at all; the sight of their retreating backsides should most certainly not be a sight to stir predatory urges in the soul of the true sportsman, who dreams of high birds and curling birds that race through the sky and then fall to earth stone dead at least a hundred yards behind him.

The connoisseurs undoubtedly have a point, and it is a point I am more inclined to appreciate whenever I think of those three birds left at High Park on my last shooting day. They were a rough shooter's birds; they were retreating rather than approaching birds

and doubtless they ran beyond the reach of Digby's feckless nose. They were not found because they were not dead when they fell and this, I suppose, is a reasonable argument against the going-away pheasant as a proper sporting target. It will not stop me pottering round my fields, each time January comes along, hoping to flush a few pheasants and lift my gun at them and put one or two of them in my bag; but I shall potter on my way in the awareness that the frequency with which retreating pheasants are wounded rather than killed is a drawback to the whole business, especially if you rely on the services of a spaniel that, even on his good days, goes searching for fallen game in a sort of confused ecstasy.

The connoisseurs have an even better point when they insist that the death of a high driven bird brings with it a drama and a beauty that the rough shooter rarely makes for himself. For the high pheasant is a fine spectacle when it flies and falls: there is the onward rush, in what seems a defiant challenge to the gun beneath; there is the bark of a single shot and the sudden change from flight to fall, with the neck thrown back in the moment of death. Once or twice in a season I am the gun who creates this spectacle, though more often the climax of the high drama is missing, since the pheasant involved in it refuses to play his – or her – part by folding his wings and descending rapidly to the earth.

There is no doubt that the high driven pheasant is, of all pheasants, the worthiest to test the shooter's swing. It is only a practised and skillful swing that manages to connect with such birds consistently. By comparison the going-away bird is aesthetically much less pleasing in his fall, which is also much less difficult to contrive. He does not descend from the sky with a sudden and startling grace that brings beauty to extinction. Often he just flops to earth and is then no more; and often too, after this unlovely flop, finding that his legs are still functional, he promptly sprints off with a turn of speed that makes you wonder why he bothered flying to begin with.

Undoubtedly there are times when the departing bird is difficult to miss; but there are other times – and here I take serious issue with the connoisseurs – there are other times when he can defeat the sharpest of shots. Let him be a strong or a wild bird; put the wind up his tail to make him dip and rock as he hurries on his way; turn him into a crossing as well as a departing bird; make him burst sharply upwards as he flies, or flush him from the top of a slope and suggest that he should sneak under the wind on cunning wings; let him burst from a tangled corner where a pheasant has never been seen before, after waiting until the man who would shoot him is on the point of breaking and unloading his gun. Advise your straightforward going-away bird to adopt one or more of these tactics and you are likely to find that he has turned into a bird that is all too easy to miss.

Very often the going-away pheasant, who is rarely shot in the head, falls wounded rather than killed. I have already acknowledged this as an indisputable drawback to the shooting of him, but although we all prefer to kill our pheasants clean, those wounded and running ones are sometimes the source of deep satisfaction. They are one of the reasons we rough shooters share our lives with wild-eyed spaniels that, for their own part, spend their days longing for the glory of the chase, the glory of a scent line that leads from field to field, from ditch to ditch, from wall to wall until at last scent turns into substance and a mired spaniel pounces in triumph upon his prize. In the days of his prime old Merlin sometimes disappeared for ten minutes at a time; more often than not he returned at last with a pheasant in his mouth. Digby is much less accomplished at this sort of thing, but just occasionally he surprises and delights me.

Over the years I have shot – and missed – many pheasants from the wrong end, most of them at High Park. They have not all been easy birds and some of them have brought me a fleeting sense of pride; but the most memorable ones have all been birds that I thought were lost to the bag and were then found at last just before the search was abandoned, found deep in the thickest tangles of the gorse or tucked up against the edges of the sike, found hiding in dense beds of brambles or whole fields away from the spot where they fell; all these most memorable birds have been a triumph for Merlin or Meg or Holly – just occasionally for Digby – rather than a triumph for me.

I am very happy to spend a day tackling difficult driven birds, although the end of the day often finds me less contented than I felt as I stood waiting for the appearance of the first bird at the beginning of the first drive. I am just as happy, perhaps even a little happier, with the sort of sport that High Park offers those of us who shoot there. There may be a chance or two at fine driven pheasants, rising from the top of Beck Bank or racing over the sike; there should be a few fast birds, not birds thirty yards high but birds that offer no more than fleeting targets as they skim the larches or appear suddenly over the near skyline. And, as Digby disobeys me in the gorse, there will probably be two or three birds that flush away from the standing guns and offer me a variety of what can loosely be classified as going-away shots.

There may be a rabbit or two as well; there may be a few woodcock and sometimes there is even the chance of a snipe; but the whole day is unlikely to bring me – or any of my guests – more than fifteen or twenty shots, and so there will not be the opportunity for much practice in the field. If we are to make our contribution to the bag we must take our chances as they come. And it is my belief that this sort of day, with not many shots and every one of them likely to be of a different sort, is in its own way just as challenging as the day that, at every drive, sends a stream of birds soaring high over the guns standing thirty or forty yards beneath them.

One Tuesday evening in the middle of January I up-ended my bucket under the old crab apple tree and sat down once more by Low Park Pond, waiting for the darkness and for any mallard that might come with it. Before settling down I had to chase a bloated and indignant muscovy duck from the water; it took to flight very unwillingly and doubtless waddled back the next morning. It is an immigrant from Brough, this muscovy, and it has taken a liking to the wheat I scatter for its wild and much lovelier cousins. It is a pest, a very greedy pest, and I have thought more than once in the past few weeks of pointing my gun at it; but I know that I should never have the heart to pull the trigger. My gun, of course, was with me the other evening; the idea of putting it to my shoulder, in order to rid myself of an obese and unwelcome presence on my flight pond, was no more than an idle fancy.

It was my first evening under the crab apple for many weeks. Whenever I have declared the pond rested and ready for another flight, whenever the edges of the water have been scattered with feathers that never belonged to a muscovy duck, whenever I have fixed in my mind an evening for Low Park Pond, then, two or three days before the appointed time, the weather has turned cold and the pond has frozen over; or I have been tied up on nights when conditions seemed ideal; or I have left the pond unfed for a week and have felt that it needed a few bucketfuls of grain before being shot again.

It was good to be back under the crab and old Merlin was very happy to be there again. I have been resting him recently and risking Digby in the field; but a quiet hour by a flight pond, with perhaps a bird or two to gather in the course of it, seemed just the thing for an ageing spaniel with stiff joints. And Digby, though I have been delighted with his recent behaviour, is not a polished retriever of duck. He has, in fact, only been flighting once, when he was determined to eat the only mallard that I shot. In those days he used to eat pheasants as well and I suspect that he would now treat his

master's duck with a little more respect; but, as long as Merlin is fit enough to go flighting, I shall take him with me and wait for the snort he always makes when he first hears the sound of wings.

It was a calm evening: too calm, I suppose, for flighting, but almost perfect for sitting under an old crab apple tree, sitting there with an old spaniel and thinking back-end thoughts about the pheasant season. The January view from my bucket was different from the view in October and November. There were no apples at my feet; there were no midges on the air, and all above me there were bare branches with just a very few withered but defiant leaves still clinging to the wood. The pond was much fuller, almost brimful; the rushes and long grass round its margins had died back. Along the line of the fence a willow had been snapped in two by the Christmas storms and was pointing jagged spikes at the sky. The gurgle of the sike was much louder than when I had last sat there listening to it. There were no crows flapping over me, though I could hear the clamour of many jackdaws two or three fields away. There were fewer sounds from pheasants, which – since well over a hundred of them had been shot – was scarcely surprising, but those fewer sounds were very noisy and very aggressive, making me think that my surviving cocks had thoughts on their mind other than the drowsy pleasures of roost.

The thoughts that occupied me on my bucket were neither aggressive nor sensual ones; they were end-of-season thoughts and they were full of satisfaction. The difference between your January thoughts, as you sit there waiting for the duck, and those that come to you on evenings in September and October, is that your January thoughts run chiefly through memories, while the thoughts of Autumn evenings are more inclined to look forward to the months ahead and to the birds that will fly through them. Early in the season you sit there smoking and waiting for the duck – you are smoking as you sit there in January as well – but as you sit there in October

your thoughts turn to the approaching pheasant-time in the hope of high birds and fast birds and the skill to shoot just a few of them. On a January evening there is more recollection than expectation, and already two or three of the memories that belong to the last few months are recognised as special and lasting ones. Each season brings just a few such, along with many very pleasant and more fleeting ones; and, although a couple of the lasting sort may still be waiting to be made, others of this same best sort, from both the present and more distant seasons, will be happy to entertain you on a calm evening in January as you sit in the failing light and wait patiently for the first mallard to fly in.

Sitting there on my bucket the other night I roamed very gratefully through my memories of a winter when High Park has rained down blessings upon me. There was the first time we shot the Gully and the last glory of the evening light as I sat smoking down by the sike at the end of it all; there was the boys' day, which was almost certainly Merlin's last full shooting day. There was the memory of his wild splendour in the gorse and of the midnight hobble that came after it. There were those December birds rising into the grey and windy sky from the top of the Gully. Only a week ago there was our first visit to the Far Pasture, with its snipe and its woodcock and its few moments of shining snow. These, I think, were the best memories of the season that has made them; these are the ones that will survive.

It was mainly memories that took possession of me as the bucket beneath me was slowly obscured by the damp rising of the night; but there were some hopes mixed in with all this recollection. There was the hope that the coming Saturday would bring just a handful of birds; there was the hope that the last day of all, a day when every normal action turns into a sort of solemn ritual, would not be entirely blank. There was a nearer hope concerned with the next half hour, for after so long without a flight I was very eager to

hear the pulse of wings again and to see the dark shapes of mallard somewhere up there in the sky. Very few came, and they came only on the edge of darkness; they were most certainly worth waiting for.

The man who shoots only in daylight misses the wonderful beauty of flighting time: a time when we seem almost to be shooting at shadows, at shadows that fly with the strength of muscled wings and with low-muttering voices. And when a shadow suddenly tumbles through the sky, you might think that you had shot a ghost, except that the splash of the shadow on the water, or the dull thump of its contact with the earth, proclaims that your prey is a thing of substance as well as of dim form. And when Merlin, who has marked the shadow's fall, bounds out to retrieve it and returns with it in his mouth, then the shadow turns into the green head and the yellow beak, into the orange legs and the pale belly of a drake mallard. It is a moment of revelation, when the eerie world of the evening flight briefly puts on both colour and flesh. It happened only once the other night; for, although four shadows flew into the pond, two of them slipped in low and slipped out even lower; and, of the two shadows that flew over me, one was already beyond my reach by the time the other was falling towards the earth.

I had forgotten, before setting out to flight, that the moon was nearing the full; even if I had remembered I should still have gone; but on a calm night under a big moon the flight is not packed into that marvellous half-hour when the remnants of the day sink into the darkness. It trickles on through hours of silver half-light and, by some mystery beyond my science, a clear sky filled with the gleam of a full moon makes the outline of approaching duck almost invisible to the flighter's gaze. Doubtless more mallard came after I had left the water and driven home, but before the season ends I shall be there once more to see what the darkness brings.

Small days with pheasants are best, and January days are incomparable: especially when they are not really days at all, but just a few hours of one, just an afternoon given over to sport after the morning has been given to very different things. My penultimate pheasant day was such a one, beginning only when I had spent Saturday morning in a classroom. It was no more than a small part of a day; it cannot have lasted more than two and a half hours, but it was worth many much longer days rolled into one. It was a richly fulfilling small portion of time and I want to explain, if I can, why it was so memorable and what it is that makes some days with the gun so much more rewarding than others.

The late start was certainly part of the pleasure. Look back through your own shooting days and I shall be surprised if you do not find that those snatched little bits of days, those days that started with something else, turning into sport only at lunchtime or even later, are among your best memories. I like my work; I enjoy writing Greek verbs on a blackboard and making boys learn them. Greek verbs are full of interest; their behaviour is strange and sometimes baffling and my life would certainly be poorer without them. But I enjoy leaving them behind me on the blackboard and holding a gun in my hand instead of a piece of chalk.

And when, last Saturday, that first cock pheasant clattered from the Gutter, very dark against the bright sky, and suddenly collapsed onto the wet earth; when Digby rushed out and gathered him clumsily and brought him half-way back to me; when I eased him from Digby's mouth while a few feathers drifted on the air; when I held the pheasant and felt his weight and admired the length of his sharp spurs; when all this was happening I enjoyed it all the more because I had come to it from a morning spent in the company of Greek verbs. It was, of course, the sense of contrast that so sharpened my pleasure: the move from intellectual, or at least mental activity, to this very different world of squelching mud and bright

sunshine and dogs and pheasants and guns. There was this sharp sense of contrast and there was also the feeling that the elements making it were somehow complementary, a feeling that Greek verbs were more appealing when I knew that pheasants would replace them as my preoccupation in the afternoon, a feeling that those same pheasants meant more to a mind that had recently been grappling with the intricacies of Greek verbs.

I love going shooting after morning school, especially when my fields are shining beneath the January sun. We have all, from time to time, defied pouring rain and found grim satisfaction beneath drenching skies. We often welcome wild winds and racing clouds for the challenge of the sport that comes with them, but I think sunshine belongs to my happiest memories of shooting days, and January sunshine is the best of all. For although there is some sadness in its brightness, shining as it does over the last weeks of another season, at the same time this gives a distinctive and memorable sharpness to the pleasures of back-end days; and, though the January sun looks down on the ending of the season, already it begins to bring longer light and it makes us think of Spring.

And, last Saturday, when we had climbed above the sike and the shadows gathered down there, when we had crossed the boundary fence and moved into my rented land, there we found sunshine in all the fields, pale sunshine under a pale blue sky with a thin little breeze stirring the tops of the gorse and the brown rushes. I shot a pheasant from the Penside gorse; it was a hen and it shone in the pale light as it flew and as it fell and then as it lay dead, lying on its back up there on the slope of the land with the breeze still ruffling its feathers. There is fire in the shine of a cock flying above you, red fire or a dark glow that sometimes deepens almost to black; but a hen shines with gleams of pale amber and white, with a subdued and suffused radiance that makes one of the subtlest beauties of days with the gun.

Two or three pheasants flushed from the Gully but they came out in the wrong places beyond the range of all three of us. Digger was pushing just too far ahead; but he behaved almost impeccably in the far pasture, where it was time for the boys to enjoy some shooting. There was a woodcock and a cock pheasant for big Jamie. Little Jamie had to be content with just a hen, while I was very content with the behaviour of my dog.

You must forgive me for filling these last pages with praise of a wild spaniel, a spaniel that would earn no praise at all from any competent trainer or handler of gun dogs; you will have to realise that, if you own a spaniel called Digger or bad Digby, and if, after you have finally decided that he is no good for shooting, he is forced back into the field because your old dog is getting too decrepit to cope with your gorse; and if on his reappearance he persuades you to change your mind by proving that he has at last turned into a dog more or less fit for service on the rough and ready days that make up most of your sport; if, moreover, all this happens to you in the course of a few weeks, then the pleasure of his company on a shooting day will be very great indeed. And your pride and pleasure in Digger's company will reach undreamed of heights if big Jamie shoots a cock pheasant that flushes from the gorse and, as soon as it falls, promptly legs it into the wood, where-upon you send Digger to find it – expecting him to fail – and are just deciding that the search will have to be abandoned when Digger, who even on his best days is an undistinguished retriever of wounded game, trots up to you with a cock pheasant lodged between his jaws.

Such moments belong to the great moments of our shooting lives, although I am getting ahead of myself in telling you of this particular moment. It belonged to the sunset on North Bank; before it happened there was a rest and a smoke at the top of the far pasture. I had remembered all my smoking gear this time and the

174

pleasure of pipe smoke was deepened by the thought that last week it had been impossible. Then there was a walk back through the fields with another pheasant for one of the boys.

Back on my own land there were no birds in the tangles of brambles and matted rushes along my boundary fence. Down in the wood the darkness was already gathering, but the sun was still on North Bank; the paleness of its afternoon shining had gone, and the

rough grass and the gorse and the margins of the wood were all glowing in its level light, while the western sky was red-rimmed and barred with orange clouds. There were birds up in the gorse. They flushed with a clatter and some flew off without a shot; but I had two hens, and then Digger flushed the cock that fell to big Jamie's shot and made my spaniel's moment of glory. There was another pheasant for little Jamie from the Gutter before it was time to finish. Then we went down the fields with eight pheasants and a woodcock in our bags, and the sky turned very pale as the sun went down, and the trees were black and bare and very sharp against the sky.

175

Pheasants crowed in the darkness of the wood. There was the beginnings of frost on the air and Digger trotted at my heels like a mud-caked shadow with long ears.

It had been an afternoon close to perfection. The sun had shone. We had shot a little more than I was expecting to shoot. We had shot well, and for my own part I had killed four pheasants with five cartridges. Digger had surpassed himself and we had gathered everything that had fallen from the sky. I had remembered my pipe and my tobacco and my matches, and there was one little pheasant day to come before the end of the season. It had been the sort of afternoon that deserved a better than average bottle of claret the same evening. As I sat in the Land Rover for a few minutes, drinking a mug of tea and munching the remains of a meat and potato pie, I already had a bottle in mind. Little Jamie rang his father on his mobile phone to find out how his shooting had gone that day. It had gone well and almost two hundred birds had been killed. I remember thinking that I would not have minded being there, but that I had almost certainly enjoyed sharing a bag of nine birds on my own shoot more than I would have enjoyed sharing a bag ten or twenty times as big on somebody else's. It would have been very difficult indeed to feel more grateful at the end of a shooting day.

I have found my old hat, the one that I lost early in September, thinking that it had fallen from my head somewhere at High Park and acknowledging finally that it was unlikely ever to be seen again. It was not at High Park; it was in my sister's cellar; and it had slipped down between a case of Meyney '88 and one of Cissac '90. I found it the other day while I was gloating over my wine (the cellar is my sister's but the wine belongs to me). I put it on my head at once and went off to look at myself in a mirror. I decided that I looked younger with my old hat on top of me; it is a worn and frayed and faded thing and doubtless it flatters the face beneath it.

I was delighted, anyway, by its reappearance and the same evening I opened my last bottle of Hortevie '86 in celebration. I was tempted to wear my hat throughout the evening; I would certainly have yielded to temptation if I had been alone. But, remembering that my sister prefers uncovered heads indoors, I put it on for the first sip or two and then put it away again. It has, of course, gone shooting with me since it returned to my life, and I have found that its presence on my head has helped to soften the sadness that always gathers over the closing days of another shooting season.

It joined me on my last flight when a friend and I shot five mallard as they flew into Low Park Pond. It was a restless evening of grey cloud and damp air and creaking branches. The duck came

early and there were more of them than I was expecting. I lost the opportunity for a right and left because, when a party of five or six came in, I spent too long watching my first target fall and telling myself that it was probably dead rather than wounded. The others had gone by the time I thought of my second barrel, but within a minute or two a high singleton came straight over me and the gun swung through him, making that wonderful moment when the shape of a duck suddenly folds its wings and falls towards the earth. In the half-darkness of flight it is – in my opinion at least – the highest beauty that comes to men who seek sport with guns: that sudden change of direction and that half-glimpsed descent through the darkening sky. The thump of contact with the earth is not a lovely sound, but it thrills the shooter, telling him that his eyes have not deceived him and that it is time for his dog to get to work. And when his old spaniel has rushed off into the marshy field behind the pond and returned within a minute or two with a drake mallard in his mouth; then, between them, the man and his dog have made one of those memories that will be slower than most to fade.

I finished the season's last flight in a mood of reverent gratitude. There was regret, of course, that the next flight was more than six months away, but there was a far deeper thankfulness for the five evenings this season that had brought me to the shadows that gather round Low Park Pond, to sit there on a bucket beneath the old crab apple tree and wait for those shapes that come dropping down to the water as the light fails.

CHAPTER EIGHT

FEBRUARY

On the first of February my hat was out with me again. It joined two of my friends in an afternoon search for a few birds to mark the end of pheasant time. I thought that my hat was certain to get very wet indeed, for it had poured down all night and the rain fell heavily all morning. From the weathermen there was no talk of an end to it before darkness, but you cannot sit indoors, cursing the cloud and the wind and the rain, on the last day of the pheasant season; you must do your cursing in the open air and put up with whatever the sky decides to fling at you. On this occasion the sky was merciful, for the rain had stopped by the time the Land Rover was chugging through Kirkby Stephen. It stayed dry right through the afternoon and we finished the season in sunshine, with yellow catkins stirring in a warm breeze that seemed to be blowing from spring.

I am a better shot with the old hat on my head. Three of our four pheasants fell to my gun and both the rabbits were mine. It was not planned to be like this; I do not invite friends to High Park so that they can stand and admire their host as he kills game with elegant efficiency. The idea is that they get most of the sport and I get a shot or two. On the last day of the season it turned out differently, but I

think Austin and Mick enjoyed themselves as we climbed the steep fields and sent our dogs into the gorse, flushing a few pheasants here and there and a few rabbits in other places. This last afternoon was, for me, a solemn performance not far removed from worship, and every moment of it was full of the whole season that it was bringing to an end. It should always be so; your last day should be a ritual of praise and thanksgiving, as you proceed from place to place and remember what each of them has given you since the first pheasant flushed from cover one morning in late October.

And so it was that, as I stood waiting to see what Digger would flush from the Gully, I thought again of those December pheasants rising into the snow, until the sudden appearance of a February pheasant jolted me back into the present just in time to kill it with my second barrel. While our dogs worked the open ground above the old pen, I remembered the November afternoon when birds had flushed so plentifully over the boys waiting for them down by the sike. North Bank was full of happy memories, for it has shot consistently well this season, and the sun came out and shone on the cock pheasant that rose into the sky and then fell to my shot as I walked along the edges of the gorse. The Gutter, the Whins, Beck Bank, the Rise: I found that every little drive had gathered new associations to itself, deepening my attachment to each little place and to High Park as a whole.

On your last shoot of the season the past hangs heavily on the damp air of the winter afternoon; everywhere you go you breathe it in and are likely to lose yourself in it, so that a bird in the present sometimes flies over you like a bird from some other time, like the memory of a pheasant rather than a pheasant with real wings. I was standing down by the sike; Austin and Mick were working their dogs through the Whins, but I was so engaged with the past, thinking back to my birthday shoot and how, standing more or less in the spot where I was standing now, I had retrieved a poor day's shooting with three pheasants and a woodcock within a minute or two; I was so full of the past that, when my friends flushed a bird and when it flew over me, I only raised my gun at the last minute and, perhaps because of this, shot the bird stone dead.

I am always half in the past on my last shoot of the season. I am also unwilling to put an end to the present and declare the season finally over. So it was that we went to the Dog-Leg and found nothing there; we tried the little planting by the duck pond and there was nothing at home. Then I dragged the three of us up to the strips above the Rise and the Gorse, where a single pheasant flushed way out of shot. Then we lined up and walked through the Hag and the Stackhole without a shot being fired. But, however long you delay the end, hunting out this place or that in the hope of another bird, you will at last have to admit that it is all over, that the whole season now belongs well and truly to the past. Hang back a little as you walk down the fields, fall behind your friends for a few minutes; and, while you turn and look back at the gorse and the firs and the larches, mutter a few words of thanks to them for everything they have given you on your shooting days during the last few months.

Remember to thank the pheasants as well and be sure, when you get home and have fed the dogs and cleaned your gun and written up your game book, be sure to pick up the phone before you start on the claret and order next year's birds.

At the beginning of this season I promised to produce, when it ended, some statistics on my performance with the gun. It is now time for me to keep this promise, but it might also be of interest to those of you who have followed the course of the season at High Park to learn the size of the bag at the end of it all. You could, of course, work it out for yourselves; but it will be much easier if I just tell you that 124 pheasants were shot and gathered, and that, when you add to these pheasants 19 mallard, 34 rabbits, 6 woodcock, one

snipe, one pigeon and one jackdaw, it all adds up to a seasonal bag of 175 head. I shall not pretend that I am not delighted.

I shall be very surprised if we ever shoot as many pheasants again, and I say this in spite of plans to build a third pen and to increase the release from 150 to 200 birds. Over the years I think the stock of pheasants has built up on the previously unshot ground that I now rent; I also think that, from December onwards, we shot into this half-wild stock and are unlikely, either next season or in the seasons that follow it, to find the Gully and the Far Pasture and those patches of gorse above the wall quite as full of pheasants as we found them this winter. It will be interesting to see how many birds come back to my hoppers during the next few weeks now that High Park has again turned into a sanctuary for pheasants rather than a place where they are killed by men with guns.

I intend, by the way, to follow a similar schedule for my shooting next season: a late October and then a mid-November day restricted to my own ground, with an outside afternoon on my rented land somewhere in between them; then a day in early December – my grand day – when we shoot the whole lot and hope for a bag of thirty birds, with a birthday shoot to follow and a New Year shoot and with the rest of January left free for sport more or less whenever I feel the urge. When I first came to High Park I used to disturb my birds too often too early in the season. It is a temptation I have now learned to resist, limiting myself to five and a half pheasant days until January comes along and tells me that the harrying time has arrived again.

Flighting has been good by my modest standards. Five flights is about right for Low Park Pond; although six, or perhaps even seven, would be possible in a season of favourable weather. I have never, by the way, seen a teal at Low Park Pond, though they often come to the secret little pond that I flighted only once because I

never found time to feed it regularly. I shall try to put this right next season; it would be good to go flighting every fortnight. Apart from the cost of bismuth cartridges, I pronounce myself well pleased with them; their effective range seems very similar to lead and I have not noticed an increased tendency to wound rather than to kill.

Woodcock were plentiful at High Park from November onwards. I expected to find that we had killed more, but they often flushed in places where no one could shoot at them or when no one was ready. Of all the birds we shoot I think woodcock the best eating. I hoard them in the deep freeze. I claim all the 'cock shot at High Park; at the end of syndicate days I beg as many of them as possible and add them to my store. I do not cook them for my friends for, as far as woodcock are concerned, I am a glutton and a selfish one; I keep my woodcock for solitary evenings, eating them two at a time with lonely relish and always honouring them with half a bottle of my best wine.

In the Autumn there were many rabbits at High Park, but disease soon took its toll. I love both shooting and eating rabbits and the season's bag has been disappointing; but there are still enough healthy rabbits to put ferrets to work and to see what sport they bring bolting from those buries along the hedges and down the sides of the Gully. Between now and the start of the trouting I hope to be out a time or two with someone else and his ferrets.

But now to the promise and its keeping, to those details of my own performance with the gun. It was a rash promise to make and there were times when I regretted it, especially after a particularly dismal performance with high pheasants high up on the edge of the Pennines. Only one of my syndicate days has been included in this book, which has been intended as a celebration of my own miniature shoot rather than as a complete record of my sport throughout the season; but the promise demands the inclusion of all my shooting

days and they have seen me on very uneven form. Anyway I find, if my arithmetic is to be trusted, that since my first flight at the end of September I have fired 285 cartridges and shot 87 pheasants, 14 mallard, 6 woodcock, 6 rabbits, 3 grouse and one jackdaw. I think this makes 117 head and so means that I have managed a ratio of one kill to something like two cartridges, which makes me what I seem to remember claiming to be when I foolishly bound myself to reveal all: a common-or-garden average shot; a man who misses plenty but generally manages to shoot well enough to avoid shame or despondency; a man who approaches a day on the margins of a friend's coverts with the reasonable hope that, at the end of the day, he will have accounted for a respectable portion of the day's bag.

I should like to be a better shot. It seems to me that there is no point in doing something unless you want to be good at it; you might, in spite of all your efforts, be forced to admit that you will never be better than run-of-the-mill, but at least the aspiration will have been there. I should like to be a better shot. I do not think that I should want ever to reach the stage when missing a pheasant or a mallard or a rabbit becomes a rare event; I think an important element of shooting lies in the acknowledgment that our quarry is often too good for us. I am not sure that our admiration for the things we hunt could survive the ability to kill almost everything at which we lift our guns: missing, in short, is an essential part of shooting. But I should still like to be a better shot. I should like, above all, to avoid those occasional days when my performance goes from bad to worse and when I end up by praying that the birds will fly over somebody else. I find such days, coming once or twice in a season, deeply dispiriting and I could get on very happily without them.

I should hone my skills on clay pigeons; it is something I used to do and it was probably wrong of me to get bored with it. I should go to a shooting school and submit myself to sessions of counselling and analysis. Perhaps, with help from the experts, I could become something of an expert myself; I might at least be able to realise what is going wrong when I have just missed a succession of birds; I might learn to climb out of failure instead of surrendering to it in hopeless gloom. It would be good to be a better shot, to be something like an expert, but I cannot help wondering if the real experts, the master-performers, relish their shooting any more than we do: those of us who tramp the fields and miss our share and shoot our share and manage, in this alternation of failure and success, to enjoy almost every minute that we spend out under the sky in pursuit of sport with the gun.

There are all sorts of jobs waiting to be done at High Park. I must attack the gorse. I must plant more trees – spruces and Scots pines and oaks and wild cherries – before the sap starts running too freely as Spring takes hold of things and gives the order to grow. And where am I going to put the third pen – probably in the strip that runs along the top of Middle Pasture – and when am I going to get round to building it? There is plenty to do and I must try to do most of it before the fishing starts and catching trout takes over my life again.

Once the fishing starts I shall never want it to end; May and June are the best months on my rivers and every year there are times in May and June when I wish they would last for ever. Once the fishing starts I shall rejoice in the spring and the summer of the year and observe with sadness how quickly they pass. At the moment it is only half-way through February and fly fishing is still over a month away; at the moment I have not properly begun thinking about fishing. My mind is still full of pheasants and duck, of banks and ditches choked with gorse and brambles and thorns, of flight ponds under the falling night, of spaniels on the rampage in cover where more sensible dogs refuse to follow.

At the moment my mind is still full of shooting; at the moment I should be tempted, if the offer came, to sacrifice the next seven months and find myself on the edge of autumn again, finding myself also on the edge of all those pleasures that come with the fading year and the falling leaves. Soon enough I shall have fallen in love with fishing again; and then I shall feel, when September comes along, that six months of the year is too short a time to spend catching trout. But, just at the moment, I should not mind waking up tomorrow and finding that it was late October and the morning of High Park's first pheasant shoot, that the time had come at last and it was the beginning of the harvest. Three months is too short a time for it and, just at the moment, I cannot wait for it to start all over again.